Parks and Gardens

A researcher's guide to sources for designed landscapes

David Lambert, Peter Goodchild and Judith Roberts

3rd edition revised by David Lambert

Landscape Design Trust in association with English Heritage

Landscape Design Trust and the authors would like to thank English Heritage for supporting this revised edition

First published by Landscape Design Trust in association with the University of York in 1991, under the title *Researching a Garden's History from documentary and published sources*
Second edition: 1995

This third edition first published by Landscape Design Trust in association with English Heritage in 2006

Written by: David Lambert, Peter Goodchild and Judith Roberts
Revised by: David Lambert

Project editor: Judith Calver
Design concept by: Andrew Shoolbred
Cover design: Justin Pursaill
Printed in the UK by Cambridge University Press

Landscape Design Trust, Bank Chambers, 1 London Road, Redhill, Surrey RH1 1LY
www.landscape.co.uk A registered UK charity no: 288510

ISBN 0951837788

British Library Cataloguing in Publication Data:
a catalogue record for this book is available from the British Library.

Contents

Acknowledgments

A guide to publications describing historic parks and gardens and the work of particular designers, the original edition of this publication was written by Janette Gallagher (now Janette Ray) and was issued in 1984 under the title *Documenting a Garden's History*. The first edition of the present publication (LDT, 1991) built on the success of the original, retaining the same purpose of offering a guide to research methods and sources, particularly where detailed historical research is required.

The second edition (1995) updated and expanded many sections and included entirely new sections on researching public parks and smaller and medium-sized sites.

The third edition has attempted to provide a summary of the rapidly expanding online resources now available to the garden-historian, to update contacts and references and to emphasise relevance to parks, cemeteries and other forms of designed landscape. The basic methodology for research, of course, remains the same, except for the additional time that can now be spent at the desk, accessing information on the internet, rather than actually in repositories.

The Ernest Cook Trust, the Garden History Society, the J Paul Getty Charitable Trust, Landscape Design Trust, the Pilgrim Trust, and the Stanley Smith Horticultural Trust helped with funding for the first edition of *Researching a Garden's History*. Amanda Arrowsmith of the Society of Archivists, Mavis Batey and Keith Goodway of the Garden History Society, Harriet Jordan of English Heritage, and John Phibbs all contributed to the revisions for the second edition. Sarah Rutherford updated the first edition's bibliography.

In preparing the third edition, the following have been very kind in helping with illustrations, commenting on updating the text and providing additional references: Charles Boot, Sarah Couch, Ian Day, Christopher Dingwall, Peter Goodchild, Fiona Green, Lorna McRobie, Barbara Simms, Steve Smith, Richard Wheeler and Jenifer White.

Finally, this booklet would not exist had it not been for the energy and support of the late Ken Fieldhouse of Landscape Design Trust, who played a leading part in publishing the first two editions and initiated work on the third.

David Lambert,
Parks Agency
May 2006

Preface

Decisions about repair, alteration, use and management of parks, gardens and other designed landscapes need to be based on a sound understanding of the design and its historic features. Research, analysis, survey and investigation are essential in this process.

Recognising the need for advice and guidance on researching these special landscapes, English Heritage welcomed Landscape Design Trust's proposal to prepare a new edition and has supported its development. The new edition will complement other publications on conservation principles and conservation management planning. English Heritage will use this guidance as a basis for commissioning and advising on historic park and garden research.

Jenifer White
Conservation Department
English Heritage
May 2006

ENGLISH HERITAGE

1 | Introduction

Since the publication of the second edition of *Researching a Garden's History* in 1995, amateur, professional and academic interest in historic gardens has continued to grow. Ten years of Heritage Lottery Fund grants have seen a transformation in all types of historic gardens, especially public parks, while restoration of parkland has become a core function of the Government's England Rural Development Programme and schemes such as the Environmental Stewardship Programme. Good practice in grant-aided schemes has established the importance of accurate historical information as the basis for conservation management plans.

Over the same ten years, the county gardens trust network has expanded; the Association of Gardens Trusts now represents 34 individual county trusts. There is now a substantial number of county surveys, both as research databases and published books.

The Journal of Garden History (now *Studies in the History of Gardens and Designed Landscapes*) and the Garden History Society's journal, *Garden History*, have been joined by others such as the *Follies Journal*, *Landscape Research* and *Landscapes* in publishing scholarly articles on garden history, and there are new university courses in the subject.

Government interest in urban parks has led to a welcome growth in awareness of their history, while English Heritage's *Power of Place* has encouraged a much more diverse and adventurous approach to identifying historic interest. The Government's *The Historic Environment: a Force for our Future* responded enthusiastically to this, referring to 'the gradual widening of the definition of what people regard as their heritage'. Since 1995 the Cadw *Register of Landscapes, Parks and Gardens of Special Historic Interest in Wales* has been completed, and the English Heritage *Register of Parks and Gardens of Special Historic Interest in England* has become far more heterogeneous, with the addition of cemeteries, allotment sites, new town landscapes and urban squares. There are also inventories for Scotland and Northern Ireland.

This richness is even greater in the survey work being carried out at a county and local level. The Government has enshrined in *Planning Policy Guidance* (PPG) 17 the principle of local authorities identifying and assessing the parks and open spaces in their area. Since 1995, awareness among English planning authorities has been encouraged by the statutory requirement that planning applications affecting registered sites be sent to the Garden History Society and English Heritage.

The need for site-specific historical research and assessment has been enshrined in the requirements of grant-givers, chiefly in the form of conservation plans and conservation management plans, advice on which is available from a number of sources (*see Chapter 3*). Historic landscape survey methodology has been described in 'An approach to the methodology of recording historic landscapes' by John Phibbs, while English Heritage's *Informed Conservation: Understanding Historic Buildings and their Landscapes for Conservation* sets out in detail the principles and practice of understanding and assessing historic places. The Department for Culture, Media and Sport *The Historic Environment, a Force for our Future* also commended management agreements and conservation plans. English Heritage has also published *Conservation Principles for the Sustainable Management of the Historic Environment* which emphasises that understanding the history of a site is one key to sustaining an historically important asset like a park or garden.

This guide introduces some of the methods and resources available for research into historic parks and gardens. It provides simple guidelines on locating, assessing, organising and presenting research material. No two areas and no two sites are the same and research methods have to be adapted accordingly, but there is likely to be a number of common procedures and starting points and these are described in the guide.

As in the previous editions, this guide identifies the diverse range of archival and published sources available for research. The value of maps, private and institutional estate papers, published and manuscript descriptions, paintings, illustrative material and photographs are all explained and key locations and repositories are identified. All sections have been revised and updated and the opportunity has been taken to respond to new lines of interest. The biggest change since 1995 has been the growth in web-based sources of information and this new edition summarises a number of the most useful.

The bibliography has again been updated and expanded. Given the increase in garden history publications in the intervening decade, it is more selective than ever. With the welcome growth in inter-disciplinary awareness, the edges of any such bibliography become blurred, so we have tried to limit the list to basic reference works. Documentary research is only one part of establishing the history of a site or the profile of sites within a county; the most important record is frequently the site itself. It is beyond the scope of this guide to deal with fieldwork in any detail, but because of its great importance, notes on fieldwork methods have been included and the references to published work on it have been expanded.

The last ten years have seen continuing growth in garden archaeology. The spectacular excavations and reconstruction of the Privy Garden at Hampton Court caught the public imagination and television interest in garden archaeology followed. At the same time, the skills of field-walking and reading the designed landscape have been disseminated among county gardens trust surveyors as well as the increasing number of landscape practices now specialising in historic landscapes. Documentary and field evidence are symbiotic – documents need to be verified by the field evidence, the field evidence needs to be interpreted with the help of the documents. Correlation of the two is vital.

2 | Practical application

Concern for historic gardens is likely to lead to practical action of one kind or another, and research should always be seen as the essential first step in this process. Thorough historical research is fundamental to establishing and understanding the development of any site and it is the base for a wide range of practical applications.

Historical research is essential:

- in establishing the evolution, designed or otherwise, of a particular site as the basis for understanding the present landscape
- in establishing sound and effective conservation policies for individual sites or groups of sites within local authority areas
- in preparing management plans to ensure the future of the site and in setting decision-making priorities
- in establishing accuracy in the conservation or restoration of planting designs
- in preparing repair or replacement schemes for structural planting and for garden buildings
- in preparing interpretative schemes and presenting sites to the public
- as the first step in an application for grant aid or for fundraising
- in unlocking other fiscal incentives such as tax relief
- in identifying the work of specific designers
- in identifying local or regional characteristics
- in understanding the technology used, for example, in creating and managing lakes, ponds and water features
- in identifying significance and tapping into other, non-expert memories and values
- in meeting the sustainability agenda, in terms of identifying environmental capital

Any form of intervention will change a site and it is vital that before any work is undertaken there should be a good understanding both of the original design of the site and of the way that the design has evolved, sometimes over hundreds of years.

3 | Research practice: county and district surveys

Recognition of the value of historic parks and gardens and the contribution they make to the wider landscape has led to more and more research work of a 'stock-taking' nature by local authorities. The Government's advice in Planning Policy Guidance (PPG) 17, that local authorities should identify and assess open space, means that many open space or green space strategies are being prepared or revised.

Changes in planning and development control requirements have also alerted local authorities to the need for basic information about the number and location of historic parks and gardens. This section outlines approaches to research work where the aim is to identify and assemble basic information on a large number of sites within a defined area such as a county, city or town, or an administrative district. This is a valuable exercise which will produce a broad picture of a whole range of parks and gardens. It will also create a substantial archive which can form the basis of detailed research on individual sites at a later stage (*see Chapter 4*). The research method outlined here can be used both in rural counties and in heavily urbanised areas.

Defining the survey area

The first task is to decide on the survey area, which will probably be determined by an administrative boundary. This is an important stage which gives a clear structure to the exercise, but it should always be remembered that larger estates, particularly in the country, frequently cross administrative boundaries.

Defining selection criteria

It is not possible to record every site which may be of historic value, and selection criteria have to be established if a survey is to be managed effectively and to stand up in planning terms. Many local or regional surveys have adapted the criteria used in the relevant national register or inventory: this is a reasonable approach given that the national lists are highly selective and omit many sites which are of local or regional importance. A number of surveys of

English Heritage's criteria for registration

English Heritage registers only those sites which it considers to be of special historic interest. As a guide to the level of historic interest required to make a site 'special' nine criteria have been drawn up against which assessment and decisions whether to register a site are made. Their application, however, must be accompanied by expert and extensive knowledge of the country's historic parks and gardens as a whole, to ensure that decisions are consistent.

The criteria are based on the assumption that the older the surviving features of a site, the rarer that type of site is likely to be, although added to this premise are other factors for consideration. Thus, types of site likely to prove of sufficient historic interest to merit inclusion on the Register are:

- Sites with a main phase of development before 1750, where at least a proportion of the layout of this date is still evident, even perhaps only as an earthwork
- Sites with a main phase of development laid out between 1750 and 1820, where enough of this landscaping survives to reflect the original design
- Sites with a main phase of development between 1820 and 1880 which is of importance and survives intact or relatively intact
- Sites with a main phase of development between 1880 and 1939 where this is of high importance and survives intact
- Sites with a main phase of development laid out post war, but more than 30 years ago, where the work is of exceptional importance
- Sites which were influential in the development of taste whether through reputation or references in literature
- Sites which are early or representative examples of a style of layout, or a type of site, or the work of a designer (amateur or professional) of national importance

- Sites having an association with significant persons or historical events
- Sites with strong group value

These criteria are not mutually exclusive categories and more than one of them may be relevant in the assessment of any particular site.

Age and registration

The first five criteria are a set of date bands, which broadly mirror the main trends in the history of the development of gardening and landscape design. Parks and gardens where the design and layout is particularly old (for a park or garden that means of the early 18th century or older) are rare, and having a set of features that is old is likely in itself to make a site sufficiently 'special' to be registered. Broadly, the more recent the structure of a garden, the more likely it is to have survived and the more common that type of site is likely still to be, so the selection process operates more selectively. For more recent sites to be of sufficient importance to be given national recognition, they have to have something in particular that makes them 'special', and here the last four criteria come into play.

Influential sites, major designers, and good standard examples

The added 'extra' could be that the park or garden has been laid out by a nationally famous designer, that it became famous or well regarded in its day, or that it had a strong influence in changing fashions. It could also be just that the site is a very good example of its type.

Associations

Close and direct associations with nationally important people or events can make a site of more historic interest than its layout alone suggests. Both the importance of the person or event, and the importance of the park or garden in relation to the person's life and work, or in relation to the event in question, are considered.

To be of relevance to registration, there must be a direct link between a site and a person or event, and this must be reflected in the actual layout of the site itself.

Group value

When a park or garden is of historic interest, but not quite of sufficient importance in its own right to merit registration, it may still be eligible for inclusion on the Register if it provides strong group value with buildings, with other land, or with a group of other registerable sites, providing this link is in itself of special historic interest. The setting of a major historic building might, for example, be carefully designed to form a piece with that building; alternatively, a garden might form an important element within a fine example of town planning. A leading designer might have laid out a related set of sites within an area, most of which are clearly of registerable quality but one of which is not so clearly so: it might still prove registerable as part of the set.

Multi-phased sites

The Register criteria can be rather misleading in suggesting that parks and gardens were usually laid out within a given date band and changed little after that. The reverse is in fact the case. The majority of parks or gardens will have developed as a series of additions or alterations as needs and fashions changed, with each phase of development varying in its impact on the landscape and its degree of interest. With such sites, it is the sum of the developments as seen in the landscape today which is considered. The value of a site can rest in the very fact that its present form is the outcome of a series of phases of development or of a more or less continuous sequence of change.

Documentation

The development of some sites is particularly well recorded in archives and published material. Where such records have survived they add to our understanding of the site and can contribute to its interest.

Taken from The Register of Parks and Gardens: an introduction, *English Heritage, 1998*

sites of county importance have recorded around ten times the number of nationally registered sites.

There are many types of historic parks and gardens: archaeological remnants, formal gardens or landscape parks associated with large houses, smaller parks and gardens of suburban villas, public parks, cemeteries, hospital grounds, town squares and walks, the planned landscapes of new towns and civic centres; and English Heritage's *Register* contains at present four historic allotment sites. *The Register of Parks and Gardens: an introduction* indicates the range of sites and the criteria for inclusion (*see page 8*). PPG17's typology of open spaces (*below*) includes many types of park, garden and designed landscape in the understanding of which historical research is essential.

The survey may aim to identify all the examples of one particular type within a given area, or there may be the more general aim of cataloguing a wide range of domestic, institutional and public sites. The scope of the exercise must be defined before work begins on gathering information. Availability of time and resources will automatically set some limits.

Preparing a storage and reference system

Research work will generate a mass of material: there will be written notes, photocopies, photographs and CDs which need to be stored and archived. Each item needs to be carefully labelled with its full reference. A simple and flexible reference system to allow easy access and updating of files should be set up.

The results of the survey are likely to be of use and to be used by a range of people, including planners, archaeologists, green-space managers, developers, environmentalists and students, as well as members of the public. They will therefore need to be adaptable for such uses: hard copy, web-based and map-based for use on the local authority's Geographical Information System (GIS). Where a survey is being carried out by or with a voluntary group, arrangements for converting results may need to be made.

Planning Policy Guidance 17 definitions for types of open space

PPG17's typology of open spaces includes many types of park, garden and designed landscape, in the understanding of which historical research is essential. Open space is defined in the Town and Country Planning Act 1990 as land laid out as a public garden, or used for the purposes of public recreation, or land which is a disused burial ground. The following typology illustrates the broad range of open spaces that may be of public value:

i)   parks and gardens – including urban parks; country parks; formal gardens

ii) natural and semi-natural urban green spaces – including woodlands, urban forestry, scrub, grasslands (eg downlands, commons and meadows), wetlands, open and running water, wastelands and derelict open land and rock areas (eg cliffs, quarries and pits)

iii) green corridors – including river and canal banks, cycleways, and rights of way

iv) outdoor sports facilities (with natural or artificial surfaces and either publicly or privately owned) – including tennis courts, bowling greens, sports pitches, golf courses, athletic tracks, school and other institutional playing fields, and other outdoor sports areas

v)   amenity green space (most commonly, but not exclusively in housing areas) – including informal recreation spaces, green spaces in and around housing, domestic gardens and village greens

vi) provision for children and teens – including play areas, skateboard parks, outdoor basketball hoops, and other more informal areas (eg 'hanging out' areas, teenage shelters)

vii) allotments, community gardens, and city (urban) farms

viii) cemeteries and churchyards

ix) accessible countryside in urban fringe areas;

x)   civic spaces, including civic and market squares, and other hard surfaced areas for pedestrians

From PPG17, Planning for open space, sport and recreation, 2002, Office of the Deputy Prime Minister

It is worth bearing in mind that electronic storage systems are subject to frequent changes: while digital copies of maps and plans, for example, are invaluable in preparing overlays, in general, hard copies should always be made or obtained, and stored in addition to digital media.

It is important to have an up-to-date base map at an appropriate scale, on which to plot identified and recorded sites (postcodes can also be useful). Entering sites on a base map will help keep track of the progress of the exercise and will identify distribution patterns. Many local authorities will require survey information to be presented in a format which will allow it to be integrated with their GIS. All Historic Environment Records – or Sites and Monuments Records – are maintained by local authorities and are going digital. There are problems with digital mapping in parks – geographical positioning systems, for example, do not work under a dense canopy of trees. The presentation of information must be agreed at an early stage.

Identifying sites

Historical maps will be a major source of information for this level of research and simple, systematic checking of all the available map sources can yield a surprising amount of information.

A systematic approach begins with the earliest available topographical surveys of the area. Many printed and manuscript town plans are invaluable in identifying the existence of open space, which was often informal but long-established, while Saxton's county plans from the early 16th century identify the existence of deer parks. The key map resource however will be Ordnance Survey (OS) maps (*see also page 25*). In rural areas, the most useful will be the six inch to one mile first and second editions; while the 25-inch scale will be especially useful for surveys of urban areas. Particularly helpful in a county or district survey is the first edition six-inch OS, on which parkland was stippled grey and is thus easily identifiable. It should be noted, however, that this is only a starting point to identifying any individual site: even by that date, some parks had shrunk in size and in any case ornamental planting often went on in the wider landscape with hill-top clumps, ornamental ridings etc. The modern map series, including the 1:25,000 and the 1:50,000 series,

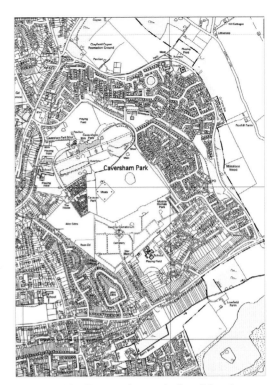

Studying parkland loss in southeast England, English Heritage prepared a 1:10,000 scale map of Caversham Park, Berkshire, using its Ordnance Survey licence, to compare change against older OS editions

will be useful particularly for rapid surveys of sites in country areas but this series is of less value in surveys of developed areas.

This method should be approached with discretion; it is always easier to pick up the larger sites in rural areas and in urban areas this method can produce far too many small sites. This information must be judged against material from other sources.

Each site should have a file into which references can be added. Each file should have a standard top-sheet, giving summary details in a standardised format. All items added to the file should be referenced with their source and date.

Printed material

In an area survey there will probably not be time to look at archival material apart from plans and some illustrations, but time should be allowed for a trawl of printed sources, many of which will be available in the local studies library. The general guides identified in Chapter 4 should be consulted and a note made of any site mentioned, together with references for future

A quick study of publications, such as guide books and authoritative volumes on designers and design styles, will help identify sites, their historic interest and other references and archive material

research. For example, Ray Desmond's *Bibliography of British Gardens* lists sites by county and is an excellent first step in identifying a potentially significant group of sites.

In addition to the standard guides, local sources and repositories should also be consulted; for example the local studies section of the library may be able to provide references to published sources on local sites and many local studies libraries have indexed further references to important local sites or to public parks. The county record office may have relevant general material listed under its subject index, while its index to maps and plans will provide useful information relatively quickly. The range of material will vary and a photocopy can often be made where appropriate and where resources allow. A reference to any printed material found should always be made and entered on the file for each site.

It should be remembered that the main aim of this level of research is to identify the location of sites, offer a summary description of historic interest, and collect basic information or references to printed and archival material. All of this can then form the basis of more detailed, site-based research in the future. At this level of survey, it is always tempting to delve deeper but the level of research and analysis has to be strictly defined by the timescale of the project.

Local knowledge

Local knowledge is always valuable: it is, for example, one of the best ways of finding out about private gardens in towns and cities and about changes which may have occurred. Local friends' groups may have a wealth of information or contacts for public parks and cemeteries. Establishing a network of local contacts is essential and should always be one of the early stages of the exercise.

However, it is wise to have a very clear idea of what information is being sought and to have a simple standard sheet on which to record notes of telephone conversations or interviews (*see Chapter 5, 'Oral sources'*). The standard record sheet should include the name of the site and its address, the name of the person being interviewed, a space for notes, the date, and a note of the person making the record. These sheets should be kept very simple but they should be completed and filed since they are part of the research and will contain information which may be consulted by other researchers in the future.

Timing is also a consideration and when contacting busy professionals or meeting with voluntary groups or local associations it is always more useful if there is something concrete to discuss. A list of information that has already been identified will be useful and of interest to others.

Recording and storing material

A county, district or metropolitan area-based survey is likely to identify a large number of potentially interesting sites, possibly running into hundreds: a search of 19th-century maps covering the Greater Manchester area identified over 300 sites, many of which have survived later periods of urban expansion. Given the potential amount of information, it is important to record data to a standard format during the project and to have a simple storage system in operation for papers and files.

The basic information to be recorded for each site will vary according to the terms of the survey, but should include the following details:

- The name of the site and/or its address
- The grid reference: a four-figure reference may be adequate for this level of recording, although six-figure references may be required for site-specific searches on internet sites. The grid letters should always be recorded

- The administrative district in which the site is located, such as the borough, district or county, and administrative boundaries. These have changed since the 19th century; this should be taken into account when searching earlier OS maps
- The size of the site

This type of search is the first step in identifying sites. The information it produces may easily be stored on a card index or on a simple database, and can be reproduced as a simple checklist quoting site name and grid reference. Supplementary material such as photocopies may be stored in a separate folder indexed by site name. The card index or database and the supplementary paper file may be referenced simply by arranging sites alphabetically by name, but the final system will depend on the reason for the survey. For example, if research is being undertaken in order to inform local authority conservation or planning decisions, it will be more effective to divide a county or metropolitan area into its administrative districts and to index sites alphabetically within these areas. The indexing system for paper files should match that used for the card index or database.

Site visits

A great deal of information can be gathered by desktop survey but a certain amount of fieldwork is an essential part of the research work. However, to cover an area as large as a county will involve high mileage, will be time-consuming and is potentially the most expensive part of the research project. Fieldwork for this kind of rapid survey should be carefully planned; visits to private sites for example will need preparatory contacts for permission.

In rural areas, travelling by car and making full use of public rights of way, it may be possible for one person to check something like eight sites in a day. This type of survey is very rapid and does not involve a detailed site visit but allows the researcher to develop a good impression of the present nature of the site and to photograph features such as lodges, gates and boundary planting. The number of sites that can be covered in a day in urban areas depends on such factors as volume of traffic: early mornings and Sundays are often the best times; a bicycle is often the most efficient way to visit a number of nearby sites.

Presentation of results

The way in which the results of the survey are presented will depend on why and for whom the survey was undertaken, and not least its budget and timetable. The most basic result, a simple printed list citing the name, location and grid reference, may be the aim, and given that several hundred sites may have been identified for the first time, can be a useful product.

If resources allow, locational information for each site, together with a short description and notes on its history from the map evidence and secondary source material, will produce a more substantial reference document. The key stages of county and district surveys are summarised in Table 1 (left).

TABLE 1: COUNTY AND DISTRICT SURVEYS: KEY STAGES

	Task	Considerations
1	Agree terms/brief	Survey area; criteria; outputs; liaison with client/steering group; timetable; arrangements for archiving
2	Prepare system	Paper/digital records; card index/ database; pro formas; storage of paper material
3	Collect survey material	Identify and visit repositories for maps; identify and visit locations for basic printed sources
4	Desktop map survey; extract material from printed sources; make local contacts; conduct interviews	Ensure efficient records system; this stage will be the most time-consuming
5	Field survey	According to brief and timetable. Visits might be identified for eg problematic sites, sample sites, major sites
6	Review	Sift material according to brief; archive what is not required for current exercise. Ensure all documents are referenced
7	Preparation and presentation of results	
8	Archive	Ensure safe storage of the study archive, eg with the county record office, the relevant local authority department, the county gardens trust, the County Historic Environment Record or Sites and Monuments Record

4 | Research practice: individual sites

This section deals with the more detailed level of research that is undertaken when researching the history and development of a single site. Levels of detail and the emphasis of the research will vary according to the overall purpose of the research, and its timetable. Historical research is an essential part of any site-specific conservation management plan, guidance on which is widely available, eg from the Countryside Agency, English Heritage and Heritage Lottery Fund. Nevertheless, the basic principles apply whatever level of detail is being investigated.

Researching the history of a park or garden from documentary and published sources can be divided

Published guidance on preparing conservation management plans stresses the importance of research to inform the care, repair and restoration of historic designed landscapes

into three general stages: preliminary work, study of documentary and published sources, and writing up.

Preliminary work

Preliminary research should include project planning and timetabling the various elements of the project. This will depend on a number of variables, and it will be helpful to be aware of the main factors to take into account, derived from a site visit and a quick check of the likely range of research material. Allowance should be made for travel, information gathering and site visits, analysis of the information and writing up. It is worth bearing in mind that only about a quarter to a third of the time should be taken up by information collection; it is always tempting to spend too long on this.

Guides to unpublished archival material

Useful references to manuscript material may be found in Colvin's *Biographical Dictionary of British Architects, 1600-1840*, the *Oxford Dictionary of National Biography*, the Royal Institute of British Architects' *Directory of British Architects 1834-1914*, and the *Victoria County Histories*. Colvin is indexed by place and personal name, and is an invaluable tool for research into historic parks as well as buildings.

The complete revised *Dictionary of National Biography* was published in 2004, with an online

---

The three stages of researching a designed landscape

Stage 1, Preliminary work
- identifying the owner and/or contact
- working out a programme for the study
- consulting the main bibliographies and guides and compiling lists of manuscript and further printed sources
- initial inquiries to major repositories and individuals, such as local historians, Friends' groups, etc
- ordering useful photocopies, photographs etc
- familiarising oneself with the site on plan and on the ground

Stage 2, Study of documentary and published sources
- searches of local archives and libraries
- searches of national archives and libraries
- recording and storing research material

Stage 3, Writing up, analysis and presentation
(this will vary according to the brief to which the researcher is working)
- an outline history of the site (the estate as a whole in general terms) up to the present
- a chronological analysis of the garden's evolution
- notes on the key individuals associated with the site
- notes on the key historic features of the site
- an assessment of present remains and condition
- a bibliography of published and unpublished sources

version in 2005. The *Victoria County Histories* are now under the direction of the Institute of Historical Research of the University of London, and new volumes continue to appear. The latest volumes contain detailed accounts of historic houses and parks, including references to archival sources. Where the *Victoria County History* is being worked on in the county, the local staff will be able to respond to inquiries. Many of the latest chapters are available online (*see Chapter 6, 'Repositories'*).

A useful means of locating manuscript material on a particular site is offered by the National Register of Archives and Chadwyck-Healey's *National Inventory of Documentary Sources*. Both have collected lists and catalogues of archives from a large number of repositories and compiled indexes to those lists. The National Register of Archives is part of the National Archives (*see Chapter 6*) and allows online searches by five indexes: business, organisations, personal, families and estates and diaries and papers. It consists of over 44,000 unpublished lists and catalogues describing archival holdings in the UK and overseas.

The Chadwyck-Healey *National Inventory of Documentary Sources* is a commercial venture producing microfiche copies of catalogues and lists of manuscript sources from archive offices, libraries and other repositories in the UK, Ireland and, in a separate series, the United States. While this is in some ways duplicating the work of the National Archives, the subject index is different and thus useful. The *National Inventory of Documentary Sources* is available at many university libraries and at the national copyright libraries (website: *www.proquest.co.uk*).

Another helpful source of information is the footnotes and references in scholarly monographs and articles in the garden history journals, ie *Garden History* (1972-; cumulative index available on the website: *www.gardenhistorysociety.org*) and *Studies in the History of Gardens and Designed Landscapes*, formerly the *Journal of Garden History*.

Finally, there may be specific guides to archival material prepared at a local level. Examples of guides to specific repositories, such as county record offices, are referred to in Chapter 6, 'Repositories'. Some of the now substantial number of books of county-based garden history include useful leads to archival sources. For example, Todd Gray's *The Garden History of Devon: an illustrated guide to sources* is an index to manuscript and published sources, while *A Survey of Historic Parks and Gardens in Herefordshire* by David Whitehead, although principally a gazetteer, likewise contains many references to manuscript material.

Guides to published material

The main bibliography for published material on garden history is Ray Desmond's *Bibliography of British Gardens*. This indispensable guide should be consulted at an early stage. Desmond's other great contribution to garden history is his *Dictionary of British and Irish Botanists and Horticulturists*, which includes plant collectors, flower painters and garden designers, and contains many references to published and manuscript sources.

Further sources can be found in a number of other bibliographies, eg Michael Holmes's *The Country House Described*; the Garden History Society bibliography, which is on the Garden History Society website; *Studies in the History of Gardens and Designed Landscapes*; *Landscape Design* (now incorporated in *Green Places*), which until 1990 produced a running bibliography of newly published work; the British Humanities Index (accessed in libraries), which since 1962 has indexed art journals including *Studies in the History of Gardens and Designed Landscapes* (and the *Journal of Garden History*) and *Country Life*; and the *Country Life Cumulative Index* (*see Chapter 6, 'Repositories'*).

Stuart Gray's *Edwardian Architecture: a Biographical Dictionary* contains bibliographical references to each entry, as does the RIBA *Directory of British Architects 1834-1914*. A number of modern scholarly editions of literary works, such as the 48-volume Yale edition of Horace Walpole's correspondence, include detailed footnotes which will contain useful references to other publications or manuscripts.

As with manuscript material, some local bibliographies can be very helpful, and are generally available at the county record office or county library. For example, *The Parks and Gardens of Cornwall* by Douglas Ellery Pett is a gazetteer with copious references to published material.

If the site is on English Heritage's *Register of Parks and Gardens of Special Historic Interest in England*; Historic Scotland's *Inventory of Gardens and Designed Landscapes in Scotland*; A *Northern Ireland Heritage Gardens Inventory*, published by the Environment and Heritage Service Northern Ireland; or Cadw's *Register of Landscapes, Parks and Gardens of Special Historic Interest in Wales*, these documents again should be checked at an early stage. Registered parks and gardens in England are mapped on the Government departments' and agencies' geographical information website for environmental schemes and designations, MAGIC,

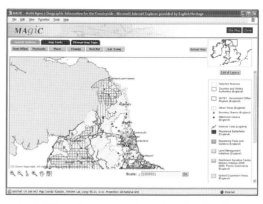

Online facilities such as www.magic.gov.uk can help identify environmental designations and schemes. This web page shows registered parks and gardens in Northumberland

and further web-based access to the English Heritage *Register* descriptions is planned for 2006-7. Copies are generally available from the agencies, or from the relevant planning authority or Historic Environment Record.

Enquiries to major repositories

An enquiry to the local record office, or a quick check of the online finding aids of the National Archives will help to establish whether a family or estate collection exists for a site. In Scotland the National Archives of Scotland and in Wales the National Library should also be checked.

Photocopies of the relevant OS plans (first or early editions of the one inch, six inch, and 25 inch, and the modern scales) can be ordered at this stage (*see Chapter 5, 'Maps and plans'*). A number of sources can be approached for these: local record office, local reference library, local authority, estate office, OS, Royal Geographical Society, British Library Map Room. Some OS maps can be printed from the internet (eg *www.old-maps.co.uk*).

The result of this preliminary research should be a list of published and unpublished sources and locations to check during the next stage of research.

To take maximum advantage of a site visit, it is worth obtaining some of the basic archival information beforehand. The first edition six-inch or 25-inch map is invaluable in reading a site for the first time; historic images, such as 18th-century Kip engravings of topographical views, are likewise extremely helpful. The site is one of

Stott Park Bobbin Mill in Cumbria has extensive areas of ancient woodland. Environmental designations such as this are mapped at www.magic.gov.uk (see above right)

the 'documents' that must be read and compared with others; several visits will probably be necessary (*see Chapter 5*, *'Fieldwork'*).

Study of documentary and published sources

Collection of research information

This stage consists of following up leads established by the preliminary work, and seeking out and taking notes from the archival and published material described in this guide; estate and family (or other owners') papers; accounts or illustrations made by visitors; maps; photographs and contemporary and modern works on history and gardening. This will involve visits to such repositories as the estate office, the county or local record office and library, a copyright library, and the London libraries and repositories; in the case of a private estate, the owner should also be consulted (*see Chapter 6*, *'Repositories'*).

It should not be assumed that all finding-aids can be checked by written, telephone or web-based inquiries. Many lists, indexes and catalogues are either only available first hand at the repository, or

need more elaborate searching than is possible by simple criteria.

At a public repository, the initial work will probably focus on those finding-aids (*see Chapter 6*). From the finding-aids and before any documents are ordered, a list of documents to be consulted should be made, including the essential information on each relevant document (brief description, date and repository location number). This will help in checking on the arrival or non-arrival of documents, and will be of particular assistance in writing up.

Despite the excitement of the chase, a systematic approach to working through finding-aids, ordering documents, and note-taking is essential. It is, for example, important always to work chronologically backwards through documents such as land tax returns or local directories (*see below*), ie always from the known to the unknown. It is worth recording more than may appear strictly relevant: the field of relevance grows as research progresses, and you may find yourself looking back on the first day's research recalling items not noted which now appear important. Any

Historic images are very helpful to researchers. This Kip engraving of Sneyd Park, Gloucestershire was made c. 1700-1710 and published in Atkyns' Ancient and Present State of Glostershire in 1712

The Chiswick House Gardens Project plan documents the chronological development of the designed landscape and its management up to the 21st century. The north vista and exedra were designed c. 1736 as part of Lord Burlington's classical gardens. The scalloped semi-circle hedge was replanted in the 1950s when the property was transferred to the Ministry of Works

information referring to items on the checklist below should be noted.

The trouble and expense of purchasing photocopies and/or photographs of whatever relevant documents a repository will allow is generally repaid: OS maps, printed county maps, articles, prints etc. Attitudes, regulations and charges vary enormously between repositories. The traditional alternative way to record a map is by

tracing, so a pad of tracing paper, or a roll which can be cut to size, should be part of a researcher's equipment. Photographs are the other alternative, and many repositories will allow them to be taken, with or without flash, although some require advance notice, and some insist that they are taken only by their approved photographer.

Organisation of collected information

It is helpful to devise some method of referencing research material as it is collected: this will be particularly useful in preparing the final report and for drawing up bibliographies and source lists. A card index or simple database can allow for easy organisation, eg by date or type of document. Storage of research material – photographs, photocopies, transcripts etc – should be systematic. As an example, the system of categorising research material shown in Table 2 (below) has proved useful.

A record of research material on index cards or database should include the site name where more than one site is being studied, type of document, date, short description and location reference. It is useful to give each document a unique title, eg reduce a map reference to author and date or a code such as 'MAP, 1888'; in the case of archival material such as bills, however, the best title might incorporate the repository's own reference number. The title recorded also on the photocopy, notes, tracing or photograph will allow for simple organisation of research findings. Always ensure that every photocopy sheet is annotated with its reference number.

One of the items of research material in the study of the historic landscape at Hawkstone, Shropshire, undertaken by the Centre for the Conservation of Historic Parks and Gardens was recorded on an index card thus:

TABLE 2: EXAMPLE OF CATEGORISING RESEARCH MATERIAL

ARC	Archival sources eg original manuscripts, letters, bills, accounts
CORR	Correspondence relating to the project
ILL	Illustrations, eg prints, drawings
LIB	Library items, eg published material such as books, journals, magazines, paintings
MAP	Maps and plans
MISC	Miscellaneous notes, eg notes on a specific topic drawn from several sources, or notes of an idea or observation for future reference
PHOT	Photographs, both old and new
SURV	Site survey notes

ROCQUE 1752   1752
"Carte topographique de la Comte de Salop ou Shropshire. Dediée:ASAR Monseigneur Le Prince de Galles" (London 1752)
British Library Maps 4900 (6)
copy at Shrewsbury Local Studies Library

Writing up

Analysis of research material

In practice, informal analysis goes on continually during the collection of research material, but there comes a time when the researcher stops collecting and concentrates specifically on analysis. Generally, this will be to establish the key phases of activity and dates for the historic layout, and to work out in detail the design, at different stages of the development (*see below*). The following are often essential exercises which incorporate material from a number of different sources:

'Naming of parts' of the site
The site will divide naturally and historically into areas of different character (parkland, different woodland blocks, pleasure grounds, kitchen garden, bowling green, bedding areas, etc). These can be broken down further where necessary and the boundaries can be drawn on a map for reference. This breakdown will prove helpful in organising research material, both during research and in presenting it. It will also assist if research is being used to formulate management policies. Names will also need to be given to individual features. Where possible, it is worth establishing through interviews the names currently used on an estate for woods, pastures etc, or the names for various areas of a public park and using these in order to avoid confusion.

Chronological table of owners, occupiers and/or managers
This can form the basis of an analysis of the phases of gardening and landscaping. The names can be put together from a number of sources both published and unpublished: *Victoria County Histories*, *Dictionary of National Biography*, Colvin, Burke's genealogies (as well as the current edition, earlier volumes are very useful), local directories, guide books, rate books, land tax returns, parish records, tithe and enclosure awards and the minutes of the relevant local government committees. The local record office catalogue to the relevant family or estate collection is likely to contain a family tree (*see Chapter 6, 'County record offices'*).

Chronological table of the development of the site
This should include: dates of the main periods of gardening activity (eg visits by designers or changes to the layout); dates for the main built and planted features; dates of descriptions by visitors; dates of the opening or the addition of new features; and the dates of chief maps and plans. Analysis of maps and plans will furnish a good deal of information which can be supplemented by the other documentary sources. Key dates may be identified from analysis of the planting on site, from a particular map, by association with a particular individual or by conclusions drawn about the succession of gardening phases. Such dates are important, eg to inform a conservation or management policy. It is

The ferny dell is a distinct character area in the Brodsworth Gardens, Yorkshire

The 1690s period-style grass and gravel cutwork parterre at Kirby Hall, Northamptonshire, is based on detailed research and scholarship of the original garden and other 17th-century designs by George London

a good idea, even if it is not required by the client, to keep an annotated copy of such a table, detailing the sources for each item.

Maps analysis

When copies of all the maps available are amassed and put in chronological order, they will show the evolution of the layout. Comparison between maps is a fascinating exercise; it is remarkable how often a map can be studied, and new details still leap out.

To bring maps to a common scale is an essential exercise. Where the maps have been digitised, this is a simple matter. In the case of hard copies, where two maps are both on generally accepted scales (eg two different OS plans), the local OS agent (*see Chapter 6, 'Ordnance Survey'*) or other skilled photocopier operator, can bring them to a common scale at the press of a button. On the other hand, where one of the maps is a manuscript estate plan, which may have an unorthodox scale or no marked scale at all, it is necessary to measure between two points, each marked on both maps, and work out the proportional difference. This can be done several times and a mean difference decided. The copy can then be enlarged or reduced by that percentage. However, it should be borne in mind that no system of photographic reproduction can avoid distortions of scale; copying and enlarging plans inevitably produces distortions of scale at a rate of about two per cent with each enlargement. This can be compensated for, to some extent, but nothing will ever quite fit, and even the simplest job comes down to interpretation.

Details from earlier maps can be sketched onto a copy of the modern 25-inch OS map as a simple way of getting an idea of what survives. It is worth having several photocopies of the 25 inch: the OS will allow four A4 copies of the modern 25 inch to be made for research purposes; for publication or any commercial return, permission needs to be gained. The modern 25 inch does have shortcomings, eg it no longer includes individual trees, but in general it is the preferable base plan.

Another essential exercise is walking the site with a copy of the OS 25 inch, and marking on it any field archaeology or notes about plants and other features (*see Chapter 5, 'Fieldwork'*).

Modern surveys

Where a full analysis of the site is required, a larger scale survey of the site as it is at present may be desirable (eg 1:500 scale). Such a survey can be produced by landscape and surveying practices using one of a variety of methods – photogrammetry from aerial photos, computerised mapping, or the more traditional use of the plane table. It should contain details of all significant trees, features and surviving field archaeology, and an analysis of existing and historic viewlines (*see Phibbs, 1983, and Chapter 5, 'Fieldwork'*).

In comparison with earlier maps, this will supply information on the historic design. An invaluable source of survey information is aerial photographs. Aerial views of individual locations are commercially available and can be sourced and ordered over the internet.

Analysis of historic planting

The evolution of planting in a designed landscape can usefully be represented in plan form. The results of the tree survey can translate into a plan showing the dates of various planted components, while a reconstruction of shrub or even flower planting in key locations can also be very useful. Lists of trees, shrubs or flowers are quite often found in archive sources but archives showing exactly where they were planted are much rarer.

In the absence of site-specific documentation, contemporary works on gardening may offer a helpful complement to what can be gleaned from documentary sources, photographs, visitors' descriptions, sale catalogues etc (*see Chapter 5, 'Other textual material'*).

Another perennial problem is finding modern equivalents to old names. In his books *Early Gardening Catalogues*, *Early Nurserymen* and *The Availability of Hardy Plants in the late 18th Century*, John Harvey offers useful sources of information on pre-1900 planting. Mark Laird's *The Flowering of the Landscape Garden* contains details of floriferous planting in 18th-century pleasure grounds, while Kim Legate's *Shrubbery planting (1830-1900)* is a valuable study of public park planting design. On 19th-century botanical nomenclature, Elwes and Henry, in *The Trees of Great Britain and Ireland*, give synonyms for the tree names they use, while Bean includes earlier names for trees and shrubs under each entry in *Trees and Shrubs Hardy in the British Isles*. Maggie Campbell-Culver's *The Origin of Plants* and Penelope Hobhouse's *Plants in Garden History* are useful summaries of plant introductions. Nomenclature is also dealt with in *European Garden Flora* and Piers Trehane's *Index Hortensis*. The *RHS Plant Finder*, published annually, is also an invaluable guide to plant-names, as well as availability. The Demeter project (*see Chapter 6, 'Repositories', English Heritage*) includes information on RHS accepted plant names as well as information on plant collections.

The planting or bedding schemes of public parks were often a subject of great civic pride and some guide books contain very full descriptions together with long plant lists which, in conjunction with photographs, can help to formulate a picture of the historic planting design.

Presentation of results

As mentioned earlier, it is important that sufficient time is allowed for analysis and writing up, tempting though it invariably is to continue collecting data.

While the brief to which a researcher works may be quite narrow and purely pragmatic, it is important for future users of a report that all analysis and conclusions are fully referenced, and that all the research material (transcripts, photographs, photocopies) is presented in an organised, accessible form. Appendices bound separately or with the report can contain full texts from estate papers, published documents, copies of all maps, photographs etc, reproduced systematically, so they can be easily referred to in the text. An alternative would be storage of clearly ordered material in a set of files or boxes.

A simple method of ordering research material for presentation is to divide it into different categories of document (*see p15, 'Organisation of collected information'*) and then arrange the documents chronologically within each category.

Archives and tree and shrub surveys can help identify the design of pleasure grounds and features such as Sir Arthur Middleton's (1838-1933) rhododendron collection at Belsay Hall, Northumberland

Another example of how to organise a body of research material is the method which was adopted by the University of York for its research on the history of Hawkstone, Shropshire.

The results were divided into four parts:

1. Introductory notes comprising:
- a short history of the park, introducing the main themes, personalities and features
- a list of the main sources of information
- a table showing the historical periods into which the history of the park may be divided
- a chronological list of guide books to the park

2. A card index of sources of information in two sections:
- repositories and collections
- individual items, organised by category of material (eg ARC, LIB)

3. An annotated subject index
An annotated list of references to individual features and aspects. This was organised as a card index, with separate cards for each feature or aspect. It contained most of the information which might otherwise have been incorporated into a full written report.

4. Notes, photocopies, photographs and tracings
These were organised by category, and stored in box files.

This system has the obvious advantage of being open ended, allowing for additions. It was devised as a means of gathering fragmentary information about individual features and aspects of the historic landscape. It also provided a method of presenting it in a way that was easily accessible to those who would be responsible for conserving and managing the property, and who would wish to know what historical information was available about individual items. In this case hand-written record cards were used, but the system could equally easily be used with a computer database.

One common method of presenting an historical analysis of a site is through a series of maps which can demonstrate quickly and clearly the changes in a site's development. For best results, maps should be brought to a common scale (*see page 20*). A series of overlays on acetate over a base plan can be an effective way of presenting such material, or printing the sequence. It can be useful to emphasise features of particular interest.

A bibliography listing all the discovered sources of published and unpublished information is a useful by-product from an historical study, and can be compiled fairly easily, provided notes have been kept during the collection of information.

Table 3 (*left*) shows a checklist of subjects to consider during the search. It indicates the range of subjects on which one might require and/or find information, and offers a framework for thinking about the research material as it is collected. It may be helpful if borne in mind during searches of documentary sources; it may also be useful during the analysis or presentation of results as a way of structuring thoughts and/or a report.

TABLE 3: SUBJECTS TO CONSIDER DURING A SEARCH

People
- Owners and occupiers
- Designers (landscape gardeners and architects, architects, amateurs, etc or, for public parks, the borough engineer or borough surveyor)
- Gardeners, estate managers, stewards, the committees responsible for the parks or cemeteries of a local authority

Dates
- Different ownerships and occupancies
- Main periods of activity
- Dates of introduction/construction of individual features
- The opening of the park and the dates of the purchase or donation of additional land

Features
- Entrance points and circulation (gates, paths, drives etc)
- Main component areas
- Landforms and earthworks
- Water features
- Planting and plants
- Buildings, constructions and ornaments

Main divisions of site
- Principal building
- Pleasure grounds
- Parkland and other land on site (eg farmland and the main functional areas of a public park such as play areas, bowling greens or pitches)
- Land beyond the site boundary but which makes an important contribution to the character of the site or its design. It is also important to note the context of a public park and its relationship with, for example, the surrounding housing development
- Kitchen garden, and other productive garden areas

Boundaries
- Past and present boundaries of the site

- the county record office and more local archival collections
- Historic Environment Record or Sites and Monuments Record
- *Country Life* magazine's picture library
- the county or local reference library
- the local museum or art gallery
- the Francis Frith Collection, Birmingham Reference Library
- the Mary Evans Picture Library
- the National Monuments Record
- the Royal Horticultural Society

(*See Chapter 6, 'Repositories' and the National Association of Aerial Photographic Libraries website: www.rspsoc.org/naplib*).

Apart from private albums, local record offices and libraries may have collections by local photographers, eg the Henry Taunt Collection in the Oxford City Library, or the Wilson Collection at King's College, Aberdeen. The local museum may also have photographic holdings deposited by local photographers or built up by the museum, and it is also worth checking with the local authority Historic Environment Record (or Sites and Monuments Record). Finally, the county reference library will have the address of the local history society, which may hold historical material, of which old photographs and postcards seem to be the most forthcoming (*see also 'Oral sources', below*).

Local photographic firms frequently made up bound collections of views or local landmarks for sale as souvenirs and these often included general

Lister Park, Bradford, from an undated postcard, in the early 20th century

views of parks or of particular features such as bandstands or spectacular floral displays. Reports of special events and ceremonies in local newspapers frequently include a photograph. The local museum or local studies library are the most likely repositories.

Public parks were a source of great civic pride and there are numerous postcard views of floral displays, general layouts and individual features. Collections may be held at the main local repositories. Local societies may be able to put researchers in touch with collections in private ownership. There are specialists dealing commercially in the sale of postcards.

Cine film can also be a useful source of information: private films may be found via the local history society, the reference library or the present or previous owners; the local television station may have some footage which can be transferred to video tape or DVD.

Lister Park, the same view after restoration in the late 1990s

A valuable source of information about parks and gardens and field archaeology is aerial photography, which divides into vertical and oblique photographs. Verticals are primarily used for producing maps; obliques can show spectacular archaeological remains. The Royal Air Force carried out a National Air Survey 1946-49: most local authorities have copies for their area, otherwise refer to the National Monuments Record for England or Scotland or the National Assembly for Wales. Copies of prints are available for purchase. Luftwaffe aerial photographs are held by the Imperial War Museum and English Heritage and photographs taken by the OS are available through the local OS map agent. There are also commercial suppliers and modern digital aerial coverage can be downloaded from the internet.

Sources of aerial photographs include:

- Historic Environment Records or Sites and Monuments Record
- Cambridge University
- National Monuments Records
- Ordnance Survey
- county councils (planning or surveyors department)

(*See also Chapter 6, 'Repositories'*)

Estate papers

Different kinds of estate need to be taken into account. In addition to the traditional private rural estate, with a main house as its focus, there are also private urban estates and those belonging to institutions such as hospitals, church authorities, educational establishments, companies, cemeteries etc. There are also public bodies such as government departments and local authorities. The distinctions between private, institutional and public estates are not always clear. The category of ownership does not always correspond to the category of use of the estate. For example, an institution such as a hospital might

The Rushmore Estate has maps, old photographs and a 1900 guide book for the Larmer Tree Grounds, Wiltshire (above), created by General Pitt Rivers for 'public enlightenment and entertainment' in 1880

be publicly owned; a traditional rural estate might be owned by a company. The general categories of 'private', 'institutional' and 'public' are helpful, however, in that they generally describe the range of ownership. In this context private ownership is taken to mean that the estate is attached to an individual or individuals for their personal use and benefit.

The term 'estate papers' covers a wide range of documentary material. They are essentially the records of the workings of the estate in such forms as the correspondence, account books, bills, inventories, working drawings, maps and memoranda of stewards, managers, owners, officers, workmen, contractors, designers and gardeners.

The range of surviving estate papers varies enormously from site to site. For example, the records of many public parks have been disposed of in the course of local government changes. On large private estates in particular, keeping full records of payments and so on was a responsibility upon which a steward's livelihood depended, and these may have been kept intact. In such cases not only will there be an account book of payments, but also bundles of 'vouchers', ie the invoices from those claiming payments from the estate. The vouchers, crumbling, dusty and unappetising though they may be (a bundle may not have been touched since the steward tied it up), contain more detail about work on the estate than any other source.

In the case of publicly owned estates (*see Chapter 6, 'Repositories'*), papers of interest will include not only those of the officers and staff involved in the running of the estate but also those of the committees which may have made policy decisions. Details of the purchase, management and design of public parks will have been recorded in the local authority committee papers, together with regular reports from the parks superintendent. Working papers illustrating details of park design, the plans of new buildings, fences or structures may have been retained or deposited by the parks department, the borough engineer's or the surveyor's department.

The committee responsible for the management of parks will probably vary throughout the history of the park – parks were often the responsibility of sanitary committees before a dedicated parks

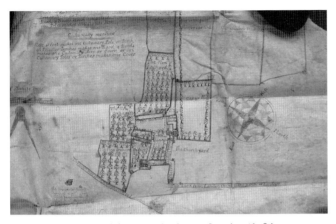

Llanellen House, Monmouthshire, an undated survey from the mid-18th century

committee was established, while capital works may have been the responsibility of a finance committee. The records of individual park keepers also occasionally survive in local archives, such as the daybook kept by Jeremiah Harrison, the keeper at Phillips Park, Manchester, in the 1840s, which is in Manchester Central Library.

Hospital and asylum records have by and large been deposited in the county record office in recent years. The minute books of the visiting committee are a valuable source of information on the construction phase, while printed annual reports provide an overview of the longer term management. A major source of information on asylums is the papers of the Metropolitan Commission in Lunacy, held at the National Archives.

For a private estate, if the estate papers are not held by the owner, they can be sought in:

- county record office and/or other local archive collections
- the family's solicitor's office: often the traditional repository for papers associated with ownership (including maps). Many solicitors make regular deposits of old papers at the county records office
- national repositories such as the Scottish Record Office or National Library of Wales
- via the National Register of Archives or National Inventory of Documentary Sources
- via other branches of the family and families of previous owners

Catalogue entries for estate collections in record offices often resort to opaque summary descriptions, eg '21 bdls _ misc. estate papers'. Such bundles can contain invaluable material, and a large collection can involve considerable research time. Some more recent catalogues, eg the Badminton Muniments (available at the Gloucestershire county record office and the National Register of Archives), include thorough descriptions of such bundles: garden history material is now being recognised by archivists as an area of research interest, but reference to it is often omitted by earlier catalogues. Much material remains unsorted, or covered only by a summary list, and where time allows for detailed research, a request can be made to search through such unsorted boxes.

Smaller houses and gardens may have been freehold, leasehold or rented from the beginning of their history or they may have changed from one category to another. They may be part of a planned estate or individual properties on their own. All of these circumstances will have an effect on the nature of any surviving documentation, the likelihood of it being traced and where it might be found. If the present and past owners or tenants can be identified, it might be possible to find their papers. They might be in a publicly accessible archive, still in the family or perhaps with a solicitor or bank. If the owner or tenant has moved from the district or if the property has had many owners or tenants from different families, it may be very difficult to trace them or living descendants.

Family and personal papers

Most catalogues distinguish between estate papers and family or personal papers. The latter comprise items such as correspondence, personal accounts, notebooks, diaries and sketchbooks. As with estate records these can vary enormously in their range, but of course they were often kept far less systematically. Again, they are sometimes summarised only in broad terms in catalogues, but, as with entries on estate papers, more recent catalogues often go into considerable detail.

Letters describing improvements on the estate, or to and from staff on the subject of the estate, are all valuable sources of information. See, for example, Brown's directions to the agent at Burton Constable in Elisabeth Hall's 'Mr Brown's Directions: Capability Brown's Landscaping at Burton Constable (1767-82)'. So, too are letters describing letters to other estates, where a correspondent was particularly gregarious. Of course, where works were particularly important the owner is more likely to have been present, reducing the chance of any written record.

Many owners kept memoranda on progress in their garden; some wrote historical notes based on archives which may now be lost. Sketchbooks are another, surprisingly common, source of valuable information.

Clues to the garden's history can also be found among such apparently unrelated personal information as subscriptions to books, membership of clubs etc, which give an idea of the owners' characters, contacts and tastes. Where no longer held by the owner, personal papers can be sought in:

- county record office and/or other local archive collections
- the family's solicitor's office
- national repositories such as the National Archives
- via the National Register of Archives or National National Inventory of Documentary Sources
- via other branches of the family and families of previous owners

Other textual material

A number of other textual archives are of use in researching a garden's history:

Bank records
The records of the private banks of the 18th and 19th centuries are generally available to researchers on submission of a written request. The principal banks at the time were Drummond's, Hoare's and Coutt's. Drummond's and Coutt's are now part of the Royal Bank of Scotland, while C Hoare & Co has its own archivist (*see Chapter 6, 'Bank archives', page 43*).

Land tax returns
These generally survive from the period 1780-1831. They include a record of the owner, occupier, acreages and land use, and are usually kept at the county records office or the National Archives.

Rate books
Although rarely complete, the run of rate books for a parish can provide a list of occupiers and owners back to a date in the second half of the 18th century. Originally part of the Quarter Sessions business, these are normally kept either in the county or borough library or county record office. As they belong with the diocesan records, they may in some cases still be held at the parish church.

Parish records
These records include the lists of births, deaths and marriages compiled by the parish church. They are normally now held at the county record office, but, as with rate books, may still be kept at the parish church.

Wills
Wills can supply useful information about an estate: many wills pre-1858 are held at the Public Record Office (*see Chapter 6, 'The National Archives'*), and now at the Principal Registry of the Family Division (First Avenue House, 42 - 49 High Holborn, London WC1V 6NP). A useful guide is provided in *Wills and their Whereabouts* by Anthony Camp.

Quarter Sessions records
These record the quarterly meetings of the County Justices from Tudor times to 1889. Particularly useful from a landscape history point of view are the land tax returns (*see above*), and the records of changes to roads and footpaths often associated with landscaping. The maps associated with highway diversions vary enormously in quality: some are the barest of sketches while others have been traced from detailed estate surveys. The records of the Quarter Sessions are usually available at the county record office, and may be indexed by parish; otherwise they are simply kept chronologically.

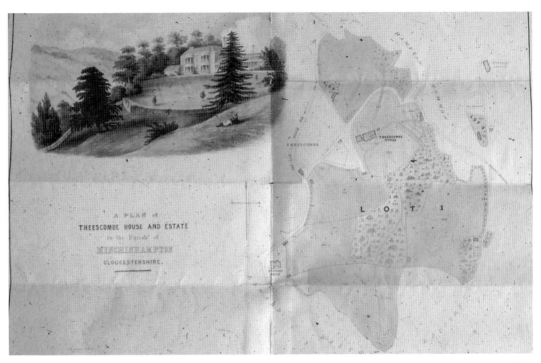

Amberley Court, Gloucestershire: view and plan from sale particulars (referring to the house under its alternative name of Theescombe Court), 1851

Manorial records

Material of particular interest may include: surveys of the parish (often in early cases a descriptive list without map); terriers (surveys of boundaries, owners and occupiers of lands); and rentals. If not deposited in the county record office, manorial papers may be held at the National Archives, which has a Manorial Documents Register.

Deeds

Deeds and other legal documents about ownership or leasehold, although relating to the estate, tend to be listed separately from estate papers in county record office catalogues. They are a useful source of information about the estate's development. AA Dibben's *Title Deeds: 13th-19th centuries* provides a guide to their interpretation. A good number of deeds will have a sketch map attached.

Sale particulars

These often contain a map (*see Chapter 5, 'Maps and plans'*), and will usually contain a more or less detailed description of the grounds, sometimes describing, for example, the make up of different woods or a descriptive list of garden buildings. Sale particulars for prestigious properties are also likely to include illustrations of some sort.

Census returns

Census returns will help in establishing the owners or occupants of a dwelling and their occupation. The census was kept from 1801 but it was not until 1841 that names as well as occupations of people were recorded. The English census records from 1851 to 1901 and births, marriages and deaths from 1837 can be viewed online or on microfilm at the Family Records Centre in London (1 Myddelton Street, London EC1R 1UW; 020 8392 5300; website: *www.familyrecords.gov.uk/frc*), and local records at local libraries or record offices. Other useful sources on occupants include ratebooks and land tax returns (*see above*), and local directories, which were compiled from the 18th century until the 1930s and give information on residents and trades. There are sets or part-sets in most local record offices and local studies libraries.

Visitors' descriptions

The literature of travel and tourism is a rich source of information about historic parks and gardens. Since the 16th century, visiting the grand houses of a region and writing descriptions of such visits has been a favoured amusement. The golden age of tours probably lay between the mid-18th and mid-19th centuries, but there are many valuable accounts dating from both before and after this time.

The most influential 18th-century tour was probably Defoe's *Tour thro' the Whole Island of England and Wales*, which first appeared in 1724-26, but which then went through eight subsequent editions, receiving extensive additions until 1779, long after Defoe's death. A different kind of tourist, but one with a keen eye for gardens, was the agriculturist Arthur Young, whose tours (1769-70) and later county surveys of agriculture are a valuable source (general views or annals of the agriculture of particular counties were widely produced by a number of writers from the late 18th century to the early 19th century). Lists of published tours appear in *The Englishman's England: taste, travel and the rise of tourism* by Ian Ousby and in Desmond's *Bibliography*.

There are lengthy lists of manuscript sources in *Reference Guide to the Literature of Travel... Great Britain* by EG Cox; *The Discovery of Britain: the English tourist, 1540-1840* by Esther Moir; and *The Search for the Picturesque: landscape aesthetics and tourism in Britain 1760-1800* by Malcolm Andrews. In *The English Garden Tour* by Batey and Lambert there is a useful list of manuscript and published tours relevant to gardens. The National Library of Scotland has a substantial collection of manuscript diaries of tours.

The gardens at Wrest Park, Bedfordshire, are described by visitors in an array of publications, such as J Beeverall's Les delices de la Grande Bretagne *(1701) and in magazines such as the* Gardener's Chronicle *(1900) and* Gardeners' Magazine *(1908)*

Tourist guidebooks to regions or to individual sites have been produced since the 18th century; the pleasure grounds of Stowe, for example, were a publishers' battleground in the mid-1700s. A plagiarised version of Benton Seeley's *Description of the gardens of Lord Viscount Cobham at Stow* (1744) was produced in the form of George Bickham's *Beauties of Stow* in 1750 and was finally trumped by Seeley with an expanded version of his book in 1759. William Gilpin's famous 'observations' on picturesque parts of the British Isles, published in the last decades of the 18th century, are perhaps the best known of numerous published tours. John Harris's *A Country House Index* has a list of guidebooks dating from 1715 to 1880 for specific country houses, which sometimes contain useful references to the grounds.

Another source of visitors' accounts of parks and gardens is the Victorian gardening magazines, which sent correspondents to see all the latest improvements. The greatest of these correspondents was probably JC Loudon, whose *Encyclopaedia of Gardening* includes a huge number of short descriptions of British gardens. Many of Loudon's descriptions, 1829-42, are included in Priscilla Boniface's *In Search of English Gardens: the travels of John Claudius Loudon and his wife Jane*. Desmond indexes a good number of the accounts in gardening magazines in his *Bibliography*.

Oral sources

The recollections of owners, occupiers, estate workers or local people, including local historians, are a valuable source of information. Living memory will cover this and most of the last century, during which major developments may well have occurred. Recollections about the estate, as well as information about current practice, are all valuable. Contacts are likely to be made via any number of channels, but these may include the estate office, the family or the local history society.

Local knowledge and the recollections of those who have worked in, managed or used a public park will be very valuable. Contacts may be made through the local authority with staff who were or still are involved in the running of the park. Other contacts may be made through groups such as the local history society, civic societies or park user groups or garden trusts. The local library will have the addresses of most groups. Any public appeal for information should be handled very carefully since it is likely to result in the return of a great deal of information, not all of which will be central to the research.

Methods of conducting such research are contained in Paul Thompson's *The Voice of the Past: Oral History*, which gives much useful advice, including the recommendation that interviews should be tape-recorded.

Published sources

Published sources are likely to contain a good deal of relevant information. Contemporary and modern works on gardening, travel, topography, local history, biography and literature, as well as contemporary and modern journals and magazines all need to be scanned for material.

Published sources may be of particular use when researching the history of a public park or the smaller private house. There was a great upsurge in popular gardening literature from the mid-19th century onwards and superintendents of parks departments may have contributed articles on the management of their own parks to national journals such as the *Gardeners' Chronicle* or have published general articles which give an insight into their views on design and management. Many professionals, such as the designers Edward Kemp, Thomas Mawson and Joshua Major, or the former superintendent of Manchester's parks, WW Pettigrew, published books in the late 19th and early 20th centuries.

Guidebooks are also an invaluable source of information about the park and its main attractions at certain periods. Some guidebooks, such as the *Souvenir of the jubilee of the opening of People's Park, Halifax* include a short history of the park and have illustrations of the main features and may include details of planting. Where there was a specialist collection, plant lists were sometimes published (eg Dean's guide to Croome Court, Worcestershire, with its accompanying plant gazetteer, *Hortus*

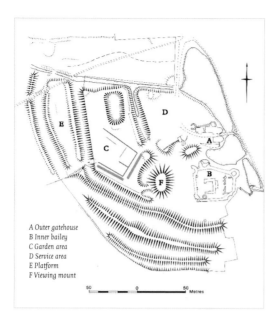

Plan of Whittington Castle grounds showing linear traces of the 14th-century garden, revealed by an English Heritage funded geophysical survey. The garden is aligned with the viewing mount

A Outer gatehouse
B Inner bailey
C Garden area
D Service area
E Platform
F Viewing mount

Croomensis, 1824) and in many cases contractors, nurseries or firms which had supplied bandstands, fountains or rockeries are either named, or advertise in the guidebook.

Many items of park furniture such as seats, benches and fountains were supplied by specialist firms which may retain catalogues or business archives: the archives and pattern books of Macfarlane's Saracen Foundry, for example, are now the property of Heritage Engineering, the specialist conservation firm, which can cast items from the original catalogues (website: www.heritageengineering.com)

Guide books often identify suppliers and manufacturers and John Davis's *Antique Garden Ornament* contains useful information on manufacturers' catalogues and repositories. Local firms may have deposited their business archives at the local record office. The Ironbridge Gorge Museums Trust has a collection of photographs and information on all major fountains and features supplied to public parks.

Local newspapers are also an important source of information. Many parks had a grand ceremonial opening which was reported together with a description, sometimes in detail, of the park.

Changes to the park or the introduction of new features such as statues or fountains will have been reported in the local press. Most local libraries have a collection of local newspapers, usually on microfilm, but the extent to which they have been indexed varies between libraries.

Articles describing individual suburban or villa gardens also occasionally appear in the gardening press although these tend to be those which have a particular horticultural interest. Magazines such as the *Gardeners' Chronicle*, and a range of other journals, may be consulted at the Royal Horticultural Society Lindley Library. Important published texts include *The Suburban Gardener and Villa Companion* by JC Loudon and *How to Lay Out a Garden* by Edward Kemp; both ran to several editions. The range of published popular works increased dramatically during the 20th century.

The rapid increase in suburban housing led to discussions between professionals on the most appropriate form of landscaping and garden design. Professional journals such as *The Builder* and *The Architects' Journal* and journals concerned with design matters, such as *The Studio*, frequently carried informative articles, many including plans of suggested designs.

Many published sources of local interest (eg parish histories, biographies of county worthies etc) will be available at the county record office and county reference library. The county inventories produced by the Royal Commission on Historical Monuments of England between 1910 and 1985 do not cover the country fully, but where a relevant volume exists it may contain useful information. No further volumes are planned. (*See also Chapter 4, 'Preliminary work' for many of the sources of help available, and 'Visitors' descriptions', above, which also refers to published sources.*)

A copyright library (ie the Bodleian Library, Oxford; British Library, London; National Library of Scotland, Edinburgh; National Library of Wales, Aberystwyth; Trinity College, Dublin; University Library, Cambridge) is of great assistance in finding old or obscure publications referred to in modern studies. Each will have different arrangements for readers and should be contacted before a visit.

Fieldwork

Documents and published sources can never give a complete or wholly reliable guide to the history of a site: illustrators exercised picturesque licence; visitors misremember details or repeat generalisations; collections of estate papers are usually fragmentary; designers' plans were rarely carried out exactly. For this reason, fieldwork is the essential complement to archival research. A skilled historic landscape surveyor would probably hold that field evidence is a more reliable source of information about what actually happened on the ground than archives.

Reading the landscape in detail is a considerable art. Elementary fieldwork, however, should be part of any researcher's work. A walk over the site with copies of old maps and illustrations can yield valuable results. Comparisons of past and present appearances can be made by locating existing features which correspond with what is shown on old documents. Given more time, further data can be collected using an old 25-inch map. Annotations from earlier maps (eg tithe or estate plan) can be sketched on to it, and any useful data noted on the plan.

Key field observations would include:

- the age of any tree stumps which can be ring counted
- the location and extent of any 'lumps and bumps' on the ground, which may indicate old drives, paths, sites of former buildings, water features, boundaries etc. Clues as to where to look may exist on historic maps
- the general character and make-up of woodlands
- any notable views, existing or partially obscured by young growth (eg gaps between old trees overlooking picturesque spots)
- the species, girth and estimated age of trees
- any indications of formal planting (old trees in straight lines other than vestigial hedgerows)
- planting intervals in any formal planting or its remains (planting intervals should be measured in Imperial, as this would have been used in the historic design)
- lodges and entrance gates and fences
- path systems and edgings
- special areas such as the playing fields, bowling greens or terraces of a public park and its main flower beds or display areas
- buildings such as the main house, or a museum, monuments, bandstand, shelters and cafeterias

This is not an exhaustive list but even such basic information will be of use when correlated with archival sources.

Leeds University scientists carrying out a survey of the complex water system at Bramham Park, West Yorkshire

6 | Repositories

A useful guide to the private and public repositories in the UK is *British Archives: A Guide to Archive Resources in the United Kingdom*, edited by Janet Foster and Julia Sheppard. On the internet, the Archon Directory, run by the National Archives (*www.nationalarchives. gov.uk/archon; see also, 'National Archives', below*), includes contact details for record repositories throughout the United Kingdom and also for institutions around the world which have collections noted under the indexes to the National Register of Archives.

Privately owned archives

In many cases, relevant documents will have been retained on site, and enquiries should be made of the owner or other contact. However, it is worth bearing in mind that he or she may be unaware of what is of potential interest; it is often best practice to visit the owner once research elsewhere has given a better idea of what to look for and enquire about, and when one has information about a range of key features, names and dates to help prompt the owner's thoughts. A working estate office is likely to contain a range of plans, including early OS maps (often the older plans have been framed and hung either here or in the house). The county archivist will often know what has been retained by the estate. Papers retained in private ownership may or may not have been listed or catalogued by the county record office, and of course special permission will be needed to view such papers.

The archives of publicly owned estates

Where a site is in public ownership, eg the National Health Service, Government agencies or local authorities, records may have been deposited at the local record office, but the owning body may have other arrangements for storing estate records, eg with the National Archives. They may be on site, in a working office or in a central archive and enquiries should be made to determine their location. For example, papers relating to public parks may have been deposited at the local record office, but it is always worth contacting the relevant local authority departments direct. Some still retain collections, often stored away uncatalogued, or they may know of the existence of papers or information elsewhere.

County record offices and other local archive repositories

County record office is used as a generic term in this guide. Most of the UK's county record offices were established around the middle of the 20th century. However, local government reorganisation since 1974 resulted in the creation of new counties and regions and some reorganisation of archive services. Metropolitan authorities may also have their own record office. Several London boroughs also have archive services.

Some university libraries have notable local and estate collections. For example, the John Rylands Library in Manchester has a great deal of material on Cheshire (University of Manchester; 0161 306 6000; website: *www.library.manchester.ac.uk*); Nottingham University Library has important material on the Duke of Portland's Welbeck Abbey and other estates (online catalogue: *www.nottingham.ac.uk/mss/catalogue*); the Bodleian has an extensive collection of Oxfordshire material (*see also, 'National Archives', below*).

There are some notable anomalies, partly resulting from reorganisation. For example, West Yorkshire's archive service has a central office in Wakefield but has district offices in Bradford, Halifax, Huddersfield and Leeds, while North and South Yorkshire have just one county record office each. Grampian is serviced by a new Regional Archive Office, but within the region the Moray District Record Office continues to function, while most of the estate collections still in Grampian are deposited at King's College Library, Aberdeen. In addition, both Scotland and Wales saw strong central repositories (ie the Scottish Record Office and the National Library of Wales) attracting deposits in advance of the founding of local repositories.

Contact details for county records offices are available from the National Archives' Archon website, or the county council website, which will also feature at the very least a general description of the collection. A preliminary telephone call (the record office will be listed under the relevant local authority) can establish whether there is a collection directly relating to the garden in question, and whether there are references in the parish or family name indexes. But even if the county record office does not contain a collection relating directly to the site being researched, it is still likely to hold material of interest: for example its collection of county and OS maps, tithe and enclosure awards and sale particulars, its library of books of county interest and its topographical collections.

Most county record offices hold the archives of their local authorities, boroughs, parishes (including tithe and enclosure awards) and manors (but for the latter see also the National Archives, below). The records of the Quarter Sessions are also often deposited at the county record office, as are land tax returns. Because the county record office is usually also used as the repository for the diocesan records, it is likely that most of the various surviving rate books will be located here (see Chapter 5, 'Other textual material'). In addition, many of the counties' businesses, firms of solicitors and landed families will have deposited their papers at the county record office. The county record office will have collected a good number of OS maps, and the earlier county

maps, as well as old and new published material on county history and topography.

Many record offices require an appointment to visit; the preliminary phone call is also valuable as a way of making contact with an archivist who may have considerable personal knowledge of the office's holdings. Most are pleased to share that knowledge, and garden researchers are often a welcome change from genealogists. However, it should be remembered that archivists are frequently imposed upon by researchers, and their job does not extend to carrying out extensive searches.

Collections of papers deposited at county record offices are usually kept intact and are accessed via catalogues, lists and indexes; there is for example likely to be an index to all the estate maps held at the office, even though they remain in separately catalogued collections. Catalogues will exist for the main collections of a record office. Each catalogue is organised by type of document (eg deeds, manorial records, estate papers, family papers, maps and plans, miscellaneous), and contains more or less detailed summaries of the documents.

It should be remembered that given the relative newness of interest in garden history, documents of garden interest may not be picked out in catalogue descriptions as thoroughly as information about other, better known interests.

The extent to which the collections of a county record office are catalogued varies greatly between offices. It is worth enquiring after any draft lists or notes on uncatalogued collections which should, with the permission of the archivist, be checked as well as the completed catalogues.

Indexes, again of greater or lesser comprehensiveness, will also have been compiled by the county record office; again these are likely to be less comprehensive than for other, longer-established areas of interest. Indexes vary between county record offices, and their scope will often depend on the interest of an archivist or local historian. They are a useful first reference but should not be relied on as a guide for a thorough search. An index to garden information in the National Archives of Scotland has been compiled by a single individual, while the Wiltshire Record

Catalogues, lists and indexes

- catalogues are detailed descriptions of organised collections (the papers of one particular family, individual or business)
- indexes are alphabetical finding aids referring to all the collections in the repository, arranged by a variety of headings, eg parish name, personal name, estate maps, illustrative material etc
- lists are summary descriptions of as yet uncatalogued collections

Office holdings have been similarly indexed by the members of the Wiltshire Gardens Trust.

Most county record offices contain at least two basic indexes to collections, by parish and by family name; there is also likely to be an index of estate maps, and a good number of offices have compiled indexes of sale particulars. There will also be a subject index, with items of interest under, for example, 'Horticulture', or 'Parks and gardens'. Where it exists, such an index is likely to be a fairly new addition to the subject headings. However, it is unlikely that items referring to a particular site will not have been found already via catalogues or the other indexes.

A particular challenge to researchers is tracing papers which, for one reason or another (eg marriage or change of ownership), are not in the record office of the county in which the site is located. Where family or land ownership or other connections to other counties are discovered, enquiries should be addressed to those record offices. Many record offices have a policy of exchanging papers and the National Archives *a2a* index (*see page 47*) includes out-county references.

County or local library services

In general terms, the county library service, run by the county council, comprises a number of branch libraries and a central library. The central library will include a reference and/or local history library, which will contain a number of useful research resources. Branch or borough libraries also often have local history material of interest. The local collection is often the pride of a county library, and is likely to have been maintained to a high standard, eg the West Country Studies Library in Exeter (01392 384216; website: *www.devon.gov.uk/index/community/libraries/localstudies*), or the William Salt Library in Stafford (01785 278372; website: *www.staffspasttrack.org.uk*).

Among the archives potentially held by the county library service are:

- topographical material (eg photographs, prints and engravings)
- manuscripts of local interest, eg papers of local

historians or worthies, scrap books or albums
- OS maps (rarely a full set but often more than the county record office)
- press cuttings
- early newspapers, often meticulously indexed
- a library of published books and pamphlets (county and parish histories), histories of the county's houses and families, and the invaluable volumes of proceedings of the county historical or archaeological society or field club – in some cases the county record office also has an excellent collection of these, as in Essex.

County or local museums

The local museum is also likely to have archives of local topographical interest, eg photographic collections, sketchbooks or other illustrative material, a remit it will share with the local art gallery which, if separate from the museum, should also be contacted about its local topographical collection. The museum may also have other archival material, eg papers of some of the local societies.

Historic Environment Records (Sites and Monuments Record)

The Historic Environment Records (HER), formerly known as the Sites and Monuments Record, are maintained by the local authorities. Each HER is a descriptive, map-based list of historic sites in the county or administrative area. Archaeological and architectural sites and structures have long been included and more recently historic parks and gardens have also appeared on several HERs. Coverage varies widely, as does the extent of information. Generally speaking, the HER will supply details of listed buildings and field archaeology (although this is often weighted towards medieval and pre-medieval finds). Garden archaeology has become an area of great interest among archaeologists and coverage of parks and gardens on HERs has significantly increased. HERs will supply printouts of maps and entries, generally for a small charge. A useful portal to HERs is supplied by the Association of Local Government

Archaeological Officers (019755 64071; website: *www.algao.org.uk*)

Local authorities

The local authority, through its planning department, parks department, conservation section or conservation officer, may have survey material on the area's gardens, or research material associated with a planning application or planning brief. Hampshire County Council's historic landscape character assessment, for example, is available online, and it is preparing its list of sites of county importance for inclusion on the website.

A full list of local and county councils can be found in the directories on *www.direct.gov.uk*

County gardens trusts

The local authority, usually county council, may also have assisted in the formation of a county gardens trust. Since 1984, some 35 county trusts have been formed. The Association of Gardens Trusts is their umbrella organisation, and can supply contact details and other information (020 7251 2610; website: *www.gardenstrusts.org.uk*).

The trusts vary widely in their activities but for most a survey of their county's historic parks and gardens is a priority. For example, the Avon trust has files on over 200 sites, each containing a map of surviving features, a brief history, a description of the site, a list of references and miscellaneous other items such as copies of prints and drawings, extracts from books and pamphlets, press cuttings etc. The Kent Gardens Trust and Kent County Council have produced a four-volume survey of the county's historic parks and gardens, completed a survey of urban parks, and one of cemeteries.

A good deal of the county trusts' survey material has been incorporated on the University of York's UK Database of Historic Parks and Gardens, and, in 2005, funding was secured to expand and complete that database in the form of a Parks and Gardens Data Partnership (*see page 51*). A significant number of trusts have been involved in publishing books on the parks and gardens of their particular county (*See Chapter 8, 'Further Reading'*).

Local history societies

The local history society may have useful material. Historical notes have often been compiled by past or present members on a wide variety of subjects. The society may also have a collection of photographs and may be able to point the researcher towards individuals with personal knowledge of a site. Its address will be obtainable from the local reference library. The proceedings of the county historical or archaeological society or field club, available in the local reference library, are also worth consulting. These are, however, often unindexed. The Local History Directory (*www.local-history.co.uk*) lists local history associations by county.

National archives

The Architectural Association
36 Bedford Square, London WC1B 3ES
(020 7887 4000)
Website: *www.aaschools.ac.uk/landscape*
The Architectural Association's course on landscape conservation, currently in abeyance, began in 1986 and amassed an impressive collection of dissertations. Recent dissertations are listed on the website.

Bank archives
Drummond's and Coutt's banks are now part of the Royal Bank of Scotland, which has a useful online guide to its archives (*www.rbs.co.uk*). This can also be obtained in hard copy for a small fee from the Royal Bank of Scotland, Regent's House, PO Box 348, 42 Islington High Street, London N1 8XL (020 7615 6127). C Hoare & Co has its own archivist (37 Fleet Street, London EC4P 4DQ; 020 7353 4522; website: *www.hoaresbank.co.uk*).

The Bodleian Library
Broad Street, Oxford OX1 3BG (01865 277000)
Website: *www.bodley.ox.ac.uk*
The Bodleian, as well as being a copyright library, has an extensive manuscript collection held in its Department of Western Manuscripts. It is recognised as a place of deposit for public records, and also contains a large number of family and personal collections, topographical drawings and

local history collections. The Gough topographical collection (1735-1809) covers the whole of England and is a particularly useful source of prints and drawings, including a substantial collection of plans by Charles Bridgeman. An index to this collection was prepared by the University of York (*see page 51*). Catalogues to published material are available online, including a preliminary catalogue of Western Manuscripts. Those seeking admission for private or commercial research must satisfy the Library that they are 'engaged on serious work for which access to our libraries is necessary, and that you will treat library material with care'. Degree and post-graduate students from other institutions need to submit proof of their status and will generally only be able to use the Library during the vacation.

Business Archives Council

6 St James's Square, London SW1Y 4LD
(020 7753 2123)
Website: www.businessarchivescouncil.com
Founded in 1934, the Business Archives Council assists in locating business records, maintains a library and produces publications. There is also a Business Archives Council (Scotland), c/o The Archives, University of Glasgow, Glasgow G12 8QQ (0141 330 6079; *www.archives.gla.ac.uk*)

The British Library

96 Euston Road, London, NW1 2DB (020 7412 7332)
Website: *www.bl.uk*
The British Library is a copyright library of printed books. Originally part of the British Museum (the British Library was formed in 1973), it has been the leading national repository for private papers since its foundation in 1753. Its Department of Manuscripts contains a vast number of personal and estate papers. Finding-aids available include the online integrated catalogue which also allows documents to be ordered (website: *catalogue.bl.uk*)

The British Library Map Library contains the best collection of OS maps available, including the Ordnance Survey Drawings (*see Chapter 5, 'Maps'*). Copies of early OS material can be bought by writing to the Map Library giving details of the site in question (a grid reference is helpful) and the dates of

maps required. Apart from a comprehensive collection of printed and manuscript maps, the Map Library also contains the George III Topographical Collection of prints and drawings, to which an index is available in the Map Room (see also MW Barley's *A Guide to British Topographical Collections and Views of the past; Topographical drawings in the British Library* by Ann Payne; and CE Wright's 'Topographical drawings in the Department of Manuscripts, British Museum', Archives vol 3 (1957), 78-87). There are catalogues to both printed and manuscript maps.

The British Museum

Great Russell Street, London WC1 3DG
(020 7323 8000)
Website: *www.thebritishmuseum.ac.uk*
The Department of Prints and Drawings contains the national collection of Western prints and drawings. There are also large documentary collections of historical and topographical prints. The Study Room is open every week day except Bank Holidays and annual closure for cleaning. Formal identity is required. Useful guides include: *The Department of Prints and Drawings in the British Museum: User's guide* by A Griffiths and R Williams; and *The Catalogue of Manuscript Maps, Charts and Plans, and of the Topographical Drawings in the British Museum,* reprint of the 1844-61 edition.

British Waterways

Llanthony Warehouse, West Quay, Gloucester Docks, Gloucester GL1 2EJ (01452 318041)
Website: *www.britishwaterways.co.uk*
The national collection of archives relating to canals and inland waterways is housed at Gloucester. The British Waterways archives include papers and maps relating to the construction and maintenance of inland waterways since the 18th century, as well as an extensive collection of photographs.

Cambridge University, Air Photograph Collection

Unit for Landscape Modelling, Sir William Hardy Building, Tennis Court Road, Cambridge CB2 1QB
(01223 764377)
Website: *www.uflm.cam.ac.uk*
The collection contains some 500,000 items dating

from 1945, including information on many historic houses and gardens. The collection is open to the public for consultation, and prints are available. An online catalogue is also available.

Cardiff Central Library
St David's Link, Frederick Street, Cardiff CF10 2DU (029 2038 2116)
Website: *www.cardiff.gov.uk/libraries*
The Central Library in Cardiff is the largest public library in Wales and one of the largest in the country. Its Local Studies Library offers a huge range of published and archival material not only on Cardiff but also on Wales generally.

Country Life
King's Reach Tower, Stamford Street, London SE1 9LS (020 7261 6337)
Website: *www.countrylife.co.uk/picturelibrary*
The magazine has one of the most important collections of photographs of houses and gardens in the country, going back to 1897, amounting to some 400,000 images. The early glass negatives, up to the 1950s, have been transferred to the National Monuments Record, but a film negative from each plate has been retained by the magazine's own library, from which prints have been made, and these are now available via its website. In addition, a cumulative index to the articles and correspondence is published annually, and is available for purchase. Many reference libraries have copies. An introduction to the collection is afforded by Brent Elliott's *The Country House Garden: from the archives of* Country Life *1897-1939*.

Courtauld Institute
Somerset House, The Strand, London WC2R ORN (020 7848 2743)
Website: *www.somersethouse.org.uk*
The Witt Library has nearly two million photographs of paintings and drawings, organised by the national schools of western tradition, eg British. They are indexed only by artist's name but where an artist is known to have visited the site or was based locally, this is a valuable resource. The Conway Library covers architecture and sculpture and includes material on houses and their landscapes.

The collection is available for consultation by members of the public, for a small registration fee. Institute staff can use the in-house database to search for particular houses.

English Heritage
Customer Services Department, PO Box 569, Swindon, Wiltshire SH2 2YP (0870 333 1181)
Website: *www.english-heritage.org.uk*
English Heritage's Heritage Protection Department maintains the *Register of Parks and Gardens of Special Historic Interest in England*. Individual site files containing materials gathered in the course of research for the Register exist; normally this will be mainly secondary material flagged up in Desmond's *Bibliography*. The Department is not a research facility or library, and will not normally undertake searches or be able to provide access to files. It will, however, endeavour to assist researchers if their work can best be taken forward with the materials it holds. Register entries and maps are available from the National Monuments Record Centre in Swindon.

English Heritage is one of the partners in the Government's MAGIC (Multi-Agency Geographic Information for the Countryside) geographical information project (*www.magic.gov.uk*), launched in 2002, which aims to bring together information on key environmental schemes and designations; it is expanding to cover the whole of the UK. English Heritage is one of the funders (with Heritage Lottery Fund, National Trust and National Trust for Scotland) of the Demeter project which records plant collections and names.

See also National Monuments Record (*see page 48*).

English Nature (Natural England, from October 2006)
Northminster House, Peterborough PE1 1UA (01733 455000)
Website: *www.english-nature.org.uk*
English Nature's work on veteran trees and on the UK Wood-Pasture and Parkland Habitat Action Plan has resulted in its gathering a significant amount of information on parks in England. In 1995 it carried out a pilot study for an inventory of parklands (*Research Report 147*). Work is ongoing, with further inventories eg Thames and Chilterns, and the East

Midlands (*Research Reports* 520 and 595), and a wood-pasture and parkland information system (*www.wapis.org.uk*) now in place, together with a web-based reporting facility. The ancient woodland inventory information is included in the MAGIC project (*see above*).

The Natural Environment and Rural Communities Bill 2005 paved the way for the merger of English Nature with parts of the Countryside Agency and Rural Development Service into a single new body, Natural England, which comes into being in 2006.

The Francis Frith Photographic Collection
Birmingham Reference Library, Central Library, Chamberlain Square, Birmingham B3 3HQ
(0121 303 4549)
Website: *www.birmingham.gov.uk/libraries*
The Frith Collection is an extensive photographic archive, and its glass negatives are housed at the City of Birmingham Reference Library. The collection contains over 330,000 subjects, including several thousand views of private and municipal parks and gardens. Over a quarter of the collection dates from 1886-1940, the rest from c. 1945-1970. The collection has been partly transferred to microfiche, and many county record offices have bought the films for their particular county. Items can be viewed on microfiche at Birmingham, and a hard copy index by place name is available and can be checked on request. Copies can be supplied for a small fee. Online information about the images can be found on the website of the Francis Frith Collection (Frith Spa, Teffont, Salisbury, Wiltshire SP3 5QP; 01722 716376; website: *www.francisfrith.com*).

Garden History Society
70 Cowcross Street, London EC1M 6EJ
(020 7608 2409)
Website: *www.gardenhistorysociety.org*
Although not a repository, the Garden History Society is the principal UK point for communication on the subject. Its journal, *Garden History*, is the main medium for new research of academic quality, and the footnotes to its articles are a rich source of information, while its newsletter and its *Register of*

Research (updated every three years) contain information on research and findings and research in progress, currently in downloadable format, although preparation of an online version is under way. Among its current projects is the publication of a new version of the Repton views contained in Peacock's *Polite Repository*.

The Hulton Getty Picture Collection
Getty Images, 101 Bayham Street, London NW1 OAG
(020 7267 8988)
Website: *www.getty-images.com*
The Hulton archive, held by Getty Images, contains some 40 million images, many of which feature everyday life from the early 20th century, including scenes in public parks. Prints and downloads can be purchased from the website.

Imperial War Museum
Lambeth Road, London SE1 6HZ (020 7416 5211)
Website: *www.iwm.org.uk*
The Imperial War Museum has an online database of collections including a photograph archive (*www.iwmcollections.org.uk*). The Print Room and Photographic Services are open by appointment.

Landscape Institute Reference Library
33 Great Portland Street, London W1W 8QG
(020 7299 4502)
Website: *www.landscapeinstitute.org*
The library has been in existence since the foundation of the Institute in 1929. The stock comprises some 5,000 reports, books and pamphlets on landscape architecture. An archive collection is being built up and currently comprises drawings and other material relating to Sir Geoffrey Jellicoe, Dame Sylvia Crowe, Sir Peter Shepheard and Michael Brown. The catalogue is online and searches can be made of the 14,000 plus drawings, slides, publications and articles in the library's database. Older items are kept off site and there is a small charge for retrieval (email: library@landscapeinstitute.org). The library is open to members of the Landscape Institute and to non-members who are *bona fide* students or researchers.

Mary Evans Picture Library
59 Tranquil Vale, London SE3 OBS (020 8318 0034)
Website: *www.maryevans.com*
This is a commercial library which since 1964 has
amassed a wide range of photographs, prints,
drawings and ephemera. Its searchable website
includes some 140,000 images, which are available
to purchase as downloads as well as hard copy.

The National Archives
Ruskin Avenue, Kew, Richmond, Surrey TW9 4DU
(020 8876 3444)
Website: *www.nationalarchives.gov.uk*
The National Archives were formed in 2003 by the
merger of the Public Record Office and the
Historical Manuscripts Commission. Established in
1838, the Public Record Office was the repository for
a wide range of public and private documents.
Among the records which may be useful to the
garden historian are: the copies of tithe maps and
awards; records of woods and forests, including the
Royal Forests; records of railway construction;
personal wills; the Close Rolls, which record deeds
of the 16th and 17th centuries; Court Rolls, which
include such manorial records as rentals, surveys
and occasional maps (when not deposited at the
county record office); all Government archives
selected for preservation; and many private and
semi-official collections of public figures, and
archives of some non-governmental organisations.
The National Archives also have a large number of
maps and plans (see *Maps and Plans in the PRO, I,
British Isles c.1410-1860*), and the staff library has a
good collection of English topographical works.

The National Archives have several helpful
search tools. The National Register of Archives
(*www.nra.nationalarchives.gov.uk/nra*) has over 44,000
lists and catalogues describing archives across the
UK and overseas, and allows online searches by five
indexes: business, organisations, personal, families
and estates and diaries and papers. Access to
Archives (*www.a2a.org.uk*) contains catalogues to
archives throughout the country, and can be
searched quickly by key words such as a site or
family name. Both the National Register of Archives
and Access to Archives are continually updated with
new lists and catalogues. The Manorial Documents
Register lists the location of manorial records.

The National Archives of Scotland
HM General Register House, Princes Street,
Edinburgh EH1 3YY (0131 535 1314)
Website: *www.nas.gov.uk*
In addition to Government and other official records,
the National Archives of Scotland (NAS), formerly
the Scottish Record Office, hold more than 450
collections of papers from private estates,
businesses and other institutions (known as Gifts
and Deposits). Scottish archives are in general terms
much more centralised than English, and the Gifts
and Deposits contain a large proportion of the family
and estate papers no longer in private custody. Maps
and plans, known as Register House Plans, are
stored separately at HM West Register House.
Searches can be made under both family and
property names, using the NAS online catalogue. A
supplementary card index of items of garden history
interest, compiled by Ms Ierne Grant, is available at
West Register House. The NAS public catalogue is
available online. The NAS also maintains the
National Register of Archives for Scotland, which
gives details of some 4,000 collections of papers still
in private hands or in regional repositories.

National Association of Aerial Photographic Libraries
c/o RCAHMS, John Sinclair House, 16 Bernard
Terrace, Edinburgh EH8 9NX
Website: *www.rspsoc.org/naplib*
Formed in 1989, the National Association of Aerial
Photographic Libraries aims to ensure the
preservation of aerial photographs of the United
Kingdom and thus the vulnerable record of the
natural and manmade landscape.

National Galleries of Scotland
Dean Gallery, 73 Belford Road, Edinburgh EH4 3DS
(0131 624 6200)
Website: *www.nationalgalleries.org*
The National Galleries Picture Library (email:
picture.library@nationalgalleries.org) holds images of
works in the galleries' collections, including many
topographical views and related material.

National Library of Scotland
George IV Bridge, Edinburgh EH1 1EW
(0131 226 4531)
Website: *www.nls.uk*
The National Library of Scotland (NLS) is
Scotland's copyright library, and also has an
important collection of manuscripts. Formed in
1925, the NLS inherited the Advocates' Library
collection which dates from the 1680s. The
Department of Manuscripts has a large number
of family and estate collections, together with
many tour journals, indexed in 1998 by the
University of York (*see page 51*). Details of most of
the NLS collections are available online.

The NLS Map Library (33 Salisbury Place,
Edinburgh), holds Scotland's most comprehensive
collection of printed maps, together with
manuscript maps and plans including
photographic versions of Roy's Military Survey
of c. 1750, which is held at the British Library (*see
page 44*). Zoomable map images of virtually all
pre-OS maps of Scotland, and of large-scale OS
town plans are now available online through the
NLS website.

National Library of Wales
Penglais, Aberystwyth, Ceredigion SY23 3BU
(01970 632800)
Website: *www.llgc.org.uk*
The National Library of Wales is the central
repository for public and private archives in Wales
as well as its copyright library. Its foundation in
1907 predated the principality's county record
offices, and many owners were successfully
encouraged to deposit papers there rather than
with the newly formed county record offices. Its
Department of Manuscripts and Records contains a
large number of estate and family collections,
while its Department of Prints, Drawings and Maps
is a rich source of illustrative and cartographic
material. In 1988, the collection of sketchbooks,
second only to the British Museum's in size, was
searched for garden material, and an index
prepared by the University of York (*see page 51*).

The National Monuments Record
National Monuments Record Centre, Kemble
Drive, Swindon, Wiltshire SN2 2GZ (01793 414600)
Website: *www.english-heritage.org.uk*
The National Monuments Record is the public
archive of English Heritage. It is divided into three
parts: archaeology, architecture and aerial
photography. The collection of aerial photography
contains some 680,000 oblique and two million
vertical photographs. The archaeological record is
primarily a computer database comprising some
400,000 records of archaeology and buildings,
with descriptions, pictures where available and
links to maps and aerial photographs. It includes
references to gardens, parks and excavations which
may include garden remains and can be browsed
online at *www.pastscape.org*. The architectural
archive contains some 1.5 million photographs,
mainly of buildings but also of garden features and
miscellaneous items: a sample can be viewed
online at *www.english-heritage.org.uk/viewfinder*.

The Images of England project
(*www.imagesofengland.org.uk*) is building up a
comprehensive database of modern photographs
of every listed building in the country, while
Viewfinder is an online browser of a number of
photographic collections such as that of the late
19th-century Oxfordshire photographer Henry
Taunt. The Garden History Society (*see above*)
passed to the archive its collection of photographs
and the microfilm of the Reefpoint collection of
Gertrude Jekyll plans held in Berkeley, California.
The late Dr Nigel Temple bequeathed his collection
of some 5,000 postcards to the National
Monuments Record in 2001 and the catalogue is
available online at *www.english-heritage.org.uk/
upload/pdf/nigel_temple_postcards.pdf* (advance
notice is necessary to view the collection, due to
archival storage).

Opening hours for the Swindon search room
should be checked: some collections are on open
access, while others can only be viewed by
appointment. A range of services is offered, some
free of charge. Online enquiry forms are available
via the website, or an information pack can be
requested by telephone.

National Monuments Record of Scotland
The Royal Commission on the Ancient and
Historical Monuments of Scotland, John Sinclair
House, 16 Bernard Terrace, Edinburgh EH8 9NX
(0131 662 1456)
Website: *www.rcahms.gov.uk*
Apart from holding Scotland's foremost collection
of photographs and drawings of its ancient
monuments and historic buildings, the National
Monuments Record of Scotland (NMRS) has an
extensive collection of other documentary and
pictorial material relating to Scotland's cultural
heritage. This includes: drawings from notable
architectural practices (such as those of Sir Robert
Lorimer and William Burn); a comprehensive aerial
photograph collection dating from the mid-20th
century; the Society of Antiquaries of Scotland's
collection of 19th-century manuscripts and
drawings; microfiche copies of the 19th-century OS
Name Books. There is an online index to the NMRS
collections, known as CANMORE (Computer
Application for National Monuments Record
Enquiries), and the website gives access to other
databases such as PASTMAP, which shows locations
and details for the listed buildings, scheduled
ancient monuments and parks and gardens on the
Scottish Inventory.

The National Monuments Record for Wales
Royal Commission on Ancient and Historical
Monuments of Wales, Crown Buildings, Plas Crug,
Aberystwyth, Ceredigion, Wales, SY23 1NJ
(01970 621233)
Website: *www.rcahmw.org.uk*
This is the principal archive for the deposit of
drawings, plans, photographs (about 500,000) and
written records of man-made structures of all
periods in Wales. It also contains the Core
Archaeological Record Index (CARN), which is
searchable online, OS record cards, and an extensive
collection of aerial photos (vertical and oblique).
CARN is being developed as the public entry-point
to the Extended National Database for Wales, a
national information resource for archaeology and
architecture, including parks and gardens.

National Museums and Galleries of Wales
National Museum and Gallery, Cathays Park, Cardiff
CF10 3NP (02920 397951)
Website: *www.museumwales.ac.uk*
The National Museum has a large holding of
watercolours, drawings, prints, sketchbooks and
albums, stored in the Prints and Drawings Study
Room. The museum website has some catalogue
information online, arranged by artist, but there are
plans to put the collections of watercolours and
drawings online shortly.

National Museums of Scotland
Chambers Street, Edinburgh EH1 1JF
(0131 247 4137)
Website, *www.nms.ac.uk*
The National Museums' holdings include the
Scottish Life Archive of photographs, documents,
postcards etc, of social interest.

Natural England, see English Nature

Ordnance Survey
Customer Services, Ordnance Survey, Romsey Road,
Maybush, Southampton SO16 4GU (02380 305030)
Website: *www.ordnancesurvey.co.uk*
The OS has a Historical Mapping Library which
contains most but not all early ('superseded') OS
maps – a number were destroyed by enemy action
during the Second World War. Orders for copies in
writing are welcome, citing details of the area and
map required (using a grid reference, or better still,
a copy of a modern map showing the site). The OS
only sells full-size copies of original sheets, on
high-quality paper, which may be over-specified for
most research purposes, at a cost of £25 and
upwards. Maps less than 50 years old are covered
by copyright law. The OS has a large collection of
aerial photographs and an air photos sales section.
Most large towns have an authorised OS agent,
who can supply the latest OS sheets and/or other
survey information.

Paul Mellon Centre for Studies in British Art
16 Bedford Square, London WC1B 3JA
(020 7580 0311)
Website: *www.paul-mellon-centre.ac.uk*
The photographic archive at the Paul Mellon Centre
has over 75,000 photographs of paintings and
drawings available for study. They are indexed only
by artist name, but where a local or itinerant
topographical artist is known to have worked in the
region of the garden being studied, an enquiry may
be worthwhile.

The Public Record Office, see The National Archives

The Public Record Office of Northern Ireland
66 Balmoral Avenue, Belfast BT9 6NY
(02890 251318)
Website: *www.proni.gov.uk*
The Public Record Office of Northern Ireland
(PRONI) was set up in 1923 to act as a repository for
official and imperial records, and also to accept
records from private depositors. It has a wide range
of family, estate, business and miscellaneous
archives (eg the Lawrence photographic collection).
The PRONI database and catalogues are not yet on
the website, but there are some helpful indexes,
including prominent persons and a parish index on
the website.

Royal Botanic Garden Edinburgh
Inverleith Row, Edinburgh EH3 5LR (0131 248 2901)
Website: *www.rbge.org.uk*
The Botanic Garden's Library (email: library@
rbge.org.uk) has a wide range of books, journals and
archives, including those related to the nursery
trade, plant-collectors, etc. The library has an
extensive collection of 19th- and 20th-century
horticultural journals.

Royal Botanic Gardens, Kew
The Library and Archives, Royal Botanic Gardens,
Kew, Surrey TW9 3AB (020 8332 5414)
Website: *www.rbgkew.org.uk/library*
The library at Kew is one of the most important
botanical reference sources in the world, with over
half a million books, illustrations, photographs,

letters and manuscripts, periodicals and maps. The
archives principally contain material relating to the
work of the Botanic Gardens, but also many
collections of the papers of botanists, gardeners and
others. The library catalogue is online but the
archives are not. There is a card index in the Archives
Room together with a number of handlists and
supplementary indexes. The archives can be
contacted direct to check their finding-aids in
relation to a particular request.

The Royal Geographical Society
1 Kensington Gore, London SW7 2AR
(020 7591 3000)
Website: *www.rgs.org*
The Society's Map Room is open to the public, and
has an almost complete set of the first and second
editions of the six-inch OS maps, and many
references to early printed maps. Within reason
(given limited staff time), photocopies are available
of the OS maps. There may be a charge to general
members of the public if they are not students.

The Royal Horticultural Society
80 Vincent Square, London SW1P 2PE
(0207 821 3050)
Website: *www.rhs.org.uk/libraries*
The Royal Horticultural Society's Lindley Library is
the most comprehensive horticultural library in the
country. Its resources include over 50,000 books
from 1514 to the present, 22,000 botanical
drawings, extensive runs of gardening magazines
and journals, including the *Gardener's Magazine* and
the *Gardeners' Chronicle* on open shelf and available for
photocopying. It also has a huge collection of
horticultural trade catalogues. It has a picture
library which can supply images from its drawings,
photographs and manuscripts collections. It has
recently acquired the Brent Elliott collection of some
5,000 postcards of municipal parks, soon to be
available online.

The RIBA Library
Royal Institute of British Architects, 66 Portland Place, London W1N 4AD (020 7580 5533)
Website: *www.architecture.com*
The RIBA Library is the largest and most comprehensive resource for information and research on all aspects of architecture. It contains a large number of items of garden interest. It has recently moved its drawings collection to the Victoria and Albert Museum's new Architecture Gallery (020 7307 3708, *www.vam.ac.uk/collections/architecture*), though its printed books, periodicals and photographic collections remain at Portland Place. The library welcomes research inquiries and has a full reprographics service. A day pass is available to the library for non-members; use of the drawings collection at the V&A is free. The online catalogue covers books, drawings, photographs, plus a biographical database of architects and an index to 300 architectural periodicals: drawings can be searched under a number of fields, and the catalogue is being updated daily. Searches can be made on request for a charge.

An attractive introduction to the garden material in the RIBA collection is Jane Brown's *The Art and Architecture of English Gardens*. More recently, RIBA has published its extensive *Directory of British Architects 1834-1914*.

The Scottish Archive Network
Website: *www.scan.org.uk*
This project is in the process of digitising millions of pages of historical records in the world's largest digitisation project, and indexing more than 20,000 collections. The website covers the contents of 52 of Scotland's major archives.

Scottish Cultural Resources Access Network
17 Kittle Yards, Causewayside, Edinburgh EH9 1PJ (0131 662 1211)
Website: *www.scran.ac.uk*
Originally developed as an educational resource, the Scottish Cultural Resources Access Network (SCRAN) contains over 300,000 images relating to Scotland's cultural heritage, drawn from a wide range of archives, museums and libraries. Among the online images available through SCRAN are those of General Roy's Military Survey of Scotland, c. 1750. Access is by subscription only.

Society of Antiquaries
Society of Antiquaries of London, Burlington House, Piccadilly, London, W1J 0BE (020 7479 7080)
Website: *www.sal.org.uk/library*
See also: Royal Museum, Chambers Street, Edinburgh EH1 1JF (0131 247 4133)
Website: *www.socantscot.org*
The Society's library is the major archaeological research library in the UK, with a fine collection of county histories and books on topography and antiquities. Its periodicals collection covers architectural history as well as the decorative arts and archaeology. Its collections of manuscripts, prints and drawings are substantial. *A Catalogue of Manuscripts in the Society of Antiquaries* by Pamela Willetts was published in 2000. The Society's collection of topographical drawings is one of the largest in the country, comprising 20,000 drawings as well as a substantial number of prints. The online catalogue at present details the books and ephemera, and indexed periodicals.

The UK Database of Historic Parks and Gardens
Landscapes and Gardens, The Department of Archaeology, University of York, The King's Manor. York YO1 7EP
Website: *www.york.ac.uk/depts/arch/landscapes/ukpg/database*
This database, set up by the University of York, currently has information on some 3,500 sites and 2,500 people, incorporating survey information from members of the Association of Gardens Trusts. The partners have recently received funding from the Heritage Lottery Fund for a three-year project to develop the resource greatly through a network of local initiatives and surveys. In its new form it will be known as the Parks and Gardens Data Partnership (PGDP), comprising three linked databases on people, places and sources.

The Victoria and Albert Museum
The Word and Image Department, Henry Cole Wing, Cromwell Road, London SW7 2RL (020 7942 8050) Website: *www.vam.ac.uk*
The Word and Image Department incorporates the former Department of Prints, Drawings and Maps. It has an extensive holding of topographical material, which is accessible via a place name (topographical) card index. This has now been copied and is available among the online catalogues. Also available is a subject index which includes entries under 'gardens'. Slides and prints are available and users are also allowed to take their own photographs. For the RIBA collections now at the V&A see under RIBA above.

Victoria County Histories of England
Institute of Historical Research, University of London, Senate House, Malet Street, London WC1 7HU (020 7862 8770)
Website: *www.englandpast.net*
The Institute of Historical Research is now the home of the Victoria County Histories. Of particular interest and value is the vast collection of slip references compiled in the late 19th century at the Public Record Office (see above) from the public records of manors and parishes: many of these have still not been used by the contributors to the VCH, and they are available for serious research at the Institute; however there is no main index, although the Institute can carry out searches for material on specific places in its archives. The website publishes a number of more recent chapters from county volumes as well as information on work in progress. It also provides details of county staff engaged in preparing current volumes who can also be contacted. In addition, each county has its own website in a consistent format, eg *www.durhampast.net*.

Sources of information about British gardens held in other countries
There are a number of repositories in other countries which hold information about British gardens and gardeners. There is no general guide to these except for: John Harris's *A Catalogue of British Drawings for Architecture, Decoration, Sculpture and Landscape Gardening, 1550-1900, in American Collections.*

Some of the American collections are well known to garden historians. For example, the Stowe papers which are at the Henry Huntington Library and Art Gallery, San Marino, California. There is a large collection of the papers of Joseph Spence (1699-1768) in the Osborn Collection at the Yale University Library, and those of Gertrude Jekyll (1843-1932) are held at the Reef Point Gardens Collection at the University of California.

Yale Center for British Art
1080 Chapel Street, PO Box 208280, New Haven, Connecticut 06520 8280, USA (203 432 2840)
Website: *ydba.yale.edu/collections*
Among the many libraries and research centres in the US which have holdings of British topographical material, the Yale Center is perhaps the best known. The Center's Department of Prints and Drawings holds more than 20,000 drawings and watercolours and 30,000 prints and is particularly strong on 18th and 19th-century artists. Inquiries can be addressed to the Curator via the address and phone number above or by email: *pdbac@pantheon.yale.edu*.

There will also be material in other European countries. For example, the papers of Russell Page (1906-1985) are kept at the Arboretum Kalmthout in Belgium (B-2920 Kalmthout, Belgium). Sometimes they can be picked up from footnotes etc in published works, or found through individuals with special knowledge, the Garden History Society, or through the web.

Visitors to the UK may have written accounts of their travels. Some have been published in English such as those of Prince Pückler Muskau (see *Tour in England, Ireland and France in the years 1828 and 1829*), and of Count Karl von Zinzendorf (see Geza Hajós, 'The Gardens of the British Isles in the Diary of the Austrian Count Karl von Zinzendorf in the Year 1768').

7 | References

Full details of all books and publications referred to in previous chapters can be found here, listed according to the chapter and section in which they are mentioned.

1 Introduction

Cadw, *Register of Landscapes, Parks and Gardens of Special Historic Interest in Wales*, 2002. Website: *www.cadw.wales.gov.uk* and *www.ccw.gov.uk*

Department for Culture, Media and Sport, *The Historic Environment: a Force for our Future*, 2001. Website: *www.culture.gov.uk/global/publications*

English Heritage, *Conservation Principles for the Sustainable Management of the Historic Environment*, 2006. Website: *www.english-heritage.org.uk*

English Heritage, *Informed Conservation: Understanding Historic Buildings and their Landscapes for Conservation*, 2001. Website: *www.english-heritage.org.uk*

English Heritage, *Power of Place*, 2000. Website: *www.english-heritage.org.uk*

English Heritage, *Register of Parks and Gardens of Special Historic Interest in England*. Website: *www.english-heritage.org.uk*

Environment and Heritage Service Northern Ireland, *A Northern Ireland Heritage Gardens Inventory*, 1992. Website: *www.ehsni.gov.uk/pubs/publications*

Phibbs, J. 'An approach to the methodology of recording historic landscapes' in *Garden History*, Volume 11:2, Autumn 1983

Office of the Deputy Prime Minister, *Planning Policy Guidance (PPG) 17: planning for open space, sport and recreation*, 2002. Website: *www.odpm.gov.uk*

Scottish Natural Heritage and Historic Scotland, *Inventory of Gardens and Designed Landscapes in Scotland*, 1997, supplementary volumes 2001 and 2003. Website: *www.historic-scotland.gov.uk*

3 Research practice: county and district surveys

Desmond, Ray, *A Bibliography of British Gardens*, St Paul's Bibliographies, 1988

English Heritage, *Register of Parks and Gardens of Special Historic Interest in England*. Website: *www.english-heritage.org.uk*

English Heritage, *The Register of Parks and Gardens: an introduction*, 1998

Office of the Deputy Prime Minister, *Planning Policy Guidance (PPG) 17: planning for open space, sport and recreation*, 2002. Website: *www.odpm.gov.uk*

4 Research practice: individual sites

Countryside Agency, *Preparing a Heritage Management Plan*, CA202, 2004

English Heritage, *Informed Conservation: Understanding Historic Buildings and their Landscapes for Conservation*, 2001

Heritage Lottery Fund, *Conservation Management Plans: helping your application*, 2004. Website: *www.hlf.org.uk/English/PublicationsAndInfo*

Guides to unpublished archival material

Brodie, Antonia; Felstead, Alison; Franklin, Jonathan, et al [Royal Institute of British Architects], *Directory of British Architects, 1834-1914*, 2 vols, Continuum, 2001

Colvin, Howard, *A Biographical Dictionary of British Architects 1600-1840*, Yale University Press, 3rd edition, 1995

Goldman, L [ed], *The Oxford Dictionary of National Biography*, Oxford University Press, 2004

Gray, Todd, *The Garden History of Devon: an illustrated guide to sources*, Exeter University Press, 1995

Whitehead, David, *A Survey of Historic Parks and Gardens in Herefordshire*, Hereford and Worcester Gardens Trust, 2001

Guides to published material

Burke's Peerage, Baronetage and Knightage, 107th edition, Burke's Peerage, London, 2003

Burke's genealogical and heraldic history of the landed gentry, 1-19 editions, Burke's Peerage, London, 1833-2005

Cadw, *Register of Landscapes, Parks and Gardens of Special Historic Interest in Wales*, 2002. Websites: *www.cadw.wales.gov.uk* and *www.ccw.gov.uk*

Desmond, Ray, *A Bibliography of British Gardens*, St Paul's Bibliographies, 1988

Desmond, Ray and Ellwood, Christine, *A Dictionary of British and Irish Botanists and Horticulturists including Plant Collectors, Flower Painters and Garden Designers*, Taylor & Francis, 1994

English Heritage, *Register of Parks and Gardens of Special Historic Interest in England.* Website: *www.english-heritage.org.uk*

Environment and Heritage Service Northern Ireland, *A Northern Ireland Heritage Gardens Inventory*, 1992. Website: *www.ehsni.gov.uk*

Gray, A Stuart, *Edwardian Architecture: a Biographical Dictionary*, Wandsworth Editions, 1988

Holmes, Michael [ed], *The Country House Described*, St Paul's Bibliographies, 1986

Lewis, WS [ed], *Horace Walpole's correspondence*, 48 volumes, Yale University Press, 1937-85

Pett, Douglas Ellory, *The Parks and Gardens of Cornwall*, Alison Hodge, 1998

RIBA, *Directory of British Architects 1834-1914*, 2 volumes, Continuum, 2001

Scottish Natural Heritage and Historic Scotland, *Inventory of Gardens and Designed Landscapes in Scotland*, 1997 and supplementary volumes. Website: *www.historic-scotland.gov.uk*

Writing up

Burke's Peerage, Baronetage and Knightage, 107th edition, Burke's Peerage, London, 2003

Burke's genealogical and heraldic history of the landed gentry, 1-19 editions, Burke's Peerage, London, 1833-2005

Colvin, Howard, *A Biographical Dictionary of British Architects 1600-1840*, Yale University Press, 1997

Modern surveys

Phibbs, JL, 'An Approach to the methodology of recording historic gardens', *Garden History* 11:2, Autumn 1983

Historic planting

Bean, WJ, *Trees and Shrubs Hardy in the British Isles*, four volumes, John Murray, 1970-1981

Campbell-Culver, Maggie, *The Origin of Plants: the people and plants that have shaped Britain's garden history since the year 1000*, Headline, 2001

Colvin, Howard, *A Biographical Dictionary of British Architects 1600-1840*, Yale University Press, 1997

Elwes, Henry John and Henry, Augustine, *The Trees of Great Britain and Ireland*, seven volumes, Edinburgh, 1906-1913

European Garden Flora Editorial Committee, *European Garden Flora*, seven titles, Cambridge University Press, 1984-2000

Harvey, John, *Availability of Hardy Plants in the late 18th century*, Garden History Society, 1988

Harvey, John, *Early Gardening Catalogues*, Phillimore, 1972

Harvey, John, *Early Nurserymen*, with reprints of documents and lists, Phillimore, 1974

Hobhouse, Penelope, *Plants in Garden History: an illustrated history of plants and their influence on garden styles – from Ancient Egypt to the present day*, Pavilion, 1999

Laird, Mark, *The Flowering of the Landscape Garden: English Pleasure Grounds 1720-1800*, Pennsylvania Studies in Landscape Architecture, 1998

Legate, Kim, 'Shrubbery planting (1830-1900)', in Fieldhouse, Ken and Woudstra, Jan [eds], *The Regeneration of Public Parks*, Routledge, 2000

RHS Plant Finder, published annually, Dorling Kindersley

Trehane, Piers, *Index Hortensis*, Timber Press, 1989

5 The range of documentary and published sources

Maps and plans

Beech, Geraldine and Mitchell, Rose, *Maps for Family and Local History: the Records of the Tithe, Valuation Office and National Farm Surveys of England and Wales, 1836-1943*, National Archives, 2004

Chubb, T, *A descriptive list of the printed maps of Somersetshire*, Somerset Archaeology and Natural History Society, 1914

Downs, RB, *British Library Resources: A Bibliographical Guide*, American Library Association, 1973; includes a list of published catalogues of estate maps

Edwards, Cliff, *Railway Records: a guide to sources*, National Archives, 2001

Harley, JB, *Ordnance Survey Maps: A Descriptive Manual*, Ordnance Survey, 1975

Kent Archives Office with Hull, Felix, *Catalogue of Estate Maps, 1590-1840 in the Kent County Archives Office*, Kent County Council, 1974

Oliver, Richard, *Ordnance Survey: a concise guide for historians*, Charles Close Society, 2nd edition, 2005

Rodger, Elizabeth M, *Large Scale County Maps of the British Isles, 1596-1850: A Union List*, 2nd edition, Bodleian Library, Oxford, 1972

Shirley, RW, *Early Printed Maps of the British Isles: a Bibliography, 1477-1650*, revised edition, Antique Atlas Publications, 1991

Skelton, RA, *County Atlases of the British Isles, 1579-1850: a Bibliography*, Carta Press, 1970

Smith, Brian, *Herefordshire Maps 1577-1800*, Logaston Press, 2004

Tate, WE, *A Domesday of English Enclosure Acts and Awards*, University of Reading, 1978

Paintings, prints and drawings

Angus, William, *The Seats of the Nobility and Gentry*, London, 1787-1807

Atkyns, Robert, *Ancient and Present State of Glostershire*, 1712

Barley, MW, *A Guide to British Topographical Collections*, Council for British Archaeology, 1974

Brewer, JN, Britton, J and Brayley, EW [eds], *Beauties of England and Wales*, 1810-16

Builder journal: there is an online catalogue of architectural plans and photographs in this and similar journals. Website: *www.york.ac.uk/inst/bihr/lists/buildingnews.pdf*

Kip, Johannes and Knyff, Leonard, *Britannia Illustrata*, 1707; topographical views of British country houses and gardens reissued by Harris, J and Jackson-Stops, G [eds], Paradigm Press, 1984

Lysons, Daniel; Lysons, Samuel, *Magna Britannia, Being a Concise Topographical Account of the Several Counties of Great Britain*, EP Publishing, 1806-22

Morris, Rev FO, *A Series of Picturesque Views of Seats of the Noblemen and Gentlemen of Great Britain and Ireland*, volumes I-VI, London, William Mackenzie, 1866-80?

Neale, J, *Views of the Seats of Noblemen* (1818-24), *Views of Seats in Scotland*, 1830, and so on

Scenery of Great Britain and Ireland in Aquatint and Lithography 1770-1860 from the Library of J R Abbey: A Bibliographical Catalogue, London, 1952

Triggs, H Inigo, *Formal gardens in England and Scotland, their planning and arrangement, architectural and ornamental features*, BT Batsford, 1902

Estate and family papers and other textual material

Alcock, NW, *Old Title Deeds*, Phillimore, 2001

Blatchford, Robert [ed], *Family and Local History Handbook*, 9th edition, Blatchford Publishing, 2005

Camp, Anthony, *Wills and their Whereabouts*, Society of Genealogists/Phillimore, 1963

Dibben, AA, *Title Deeds, 13th-19th centuries*, Historical Association, 1990

Hall, Elisabeth, 'Mr Brown's Directions: Capability Brown's Landscaping at Burton Constable (1767-82)', *Garden History* 23:2, 1995

Visitors' descriptions

Andrews, Malcolm, *The Search for the Picturesque: landscape aesthetics and tourism in Britain, 1760-1800*, Scholar Press, 1989

Batey, Mavis and Lambert, David, *The English Garden Tour*, John Murray, 1990

Bickham, George, *The Beauties of Stow: or, a Description of the Pleasant Seat, and Noble Gardens, of the Right Honourable Lord Viscount Cobham*, London, E Owen for George Bickham, 1750

Boniface, Priscilla [ed], *In Search of English Gardens: the travels of John Claudius Loudon and his wife Jane*, Lennard Publishing, 1987

Cox, EG, *Reference Guide to the Literature of Travel... Great Britain*, vol.iii, Seattle, 1949

Defoe, Daniel, *A Tour thro' the whole island of Great Britain, divided into Circuits or Journeys. Giving a particular and diverting account of whatever is Curious and worth Observation, Particularly fitted for the reading of such as desire to travel over the island*, London, Peter Davies, 1929

Gilpin, William, *Observations relative chiefly to Picturesque Beauty, made in the year 1772, on several parts of England, particularly The Mountains and Lakes of Cumberland and Westmorland*, second edition, two volumes, 1788 (Gilpin's first observation has recently been reissued: *Observations on the River Wye*, Pallas Athene Publishers, 2005)

Harris, John, *A Country House Index*, Pinhorns, Isle of Wight, 1971

Loudon, John Claudius, *An Encyclopaedia of Gardening*, London, 1822

Moir, Esther, *The Discovery of Britain: The English tourists, 1540-1840*, Routledge & Kegan Paul, 1964

Mitchell, Arthur, *Lists of Travels and Tours in Scotland, 1296 to 1900*, Edinburgh, 1902

Ousby, Ian, *The Englishman's England: taste, travel and the rise of tourism*, Cambridge University Press, 1990

Seeley, Benton, *A description of the Gardens at Stowe*, 1744, with further expanded editions and additional maps and engravings from 1745 to 1763

Young, Arthur, *Tours in England and Wales*, selected from the *Annals of Agriculture*, available online. Website: *www.visionofbritain.org.uk/text*

Oral sources
Thompson, Paul, *The Voice of the Past: Oral History*, Oxford University Press, 2000

Published sources
Davis, John, *Antique Garden Ornament*, Antique Collectors Club, 1991

Dean, W, *Hortus Croomensis*, a guide to Croome Court, Worcestershire, with an accompanying plant gazetteer, 1824

Kemp, Edward, *How to Lay Out a Garden*, 1850

Kemp, Edward, *The Parks and Gardens of London*, 1850

Loudon, JC, *The suburban Gardener and Villa companion*, 1838, revised in 1850 as *The Villa Gardener*

Lynon, EW for the County Borough of Halifax, *Souvenir of the jubilee of the opening of People's Park, Halifax, West Yorkshire*, Souvenir booklet, 1907

Mawson, Thomas, *Art and craft of garden making*, 3rd edition, 1907

Pettigrew, WW, books include: *Municipal Parks: Layout, Management and Administration*, 1937

6 Repositories

Archon Directory, run by the National Archives, *www.nationalarchives.gov.uk/archon*

Foster, Janet and Sheppard, Julia [eds], *British Archives: A Guide to Archive Resources in the United Kingdom*, Palgrave Macmillan, 2002

Local authorities
Hampshire County Council historic landscape character assessment, website: *www.hants.gov.uk/landscape*. Hampshire sites of county importance online at: *www.hants.gov.uk/environment/hpg*

British Library
Barley, MW, *A Guide to British Topographical Collections*, Council for British Archaeology, 1974

Payne, Ann, *Views of the past: topographical drawings in the British Library*, London, 1987

Wright, CE, 'Topographical drawings in the Department of Manuscripts, British Museum', *Archives* vol 3 (1957), 78-87

British Museum
Griffiths, Antony and Williams, Reginald, *The Department of Prints and Drawings in the British Museum: User's guide*, British Museum Publications, 1987

The Catalogue of Manuscript Maps, Charts and Plans, and of the Topographical Drawings in the British Museum, reprint of the 1844-61 edition, Gregg Associates, Brussels, 1962; now also on CD

Country Life
Brent Elliott's *The Country House Garden: from the archives of Country Life 1897-1939*, London, 1995

National Archive
Maps and Plans in the PRO, I, British Isles c.1410-1860, HMSO, 1967

RIBA
Brown, Jane, *The Art and Architecture of English Gardens*, Weidenfeld & Nicolson, 1989

RIBA, *Directory of British Architects 1834-1914*, two volumes, Continuum, 2001

Society of Antiquaries
Willets, Pamela, *Catalogue of manuscripts in the Society of Antiquaries of London*, Brewer, DS for the Society of Antiquaries of London, 2000

Other countries
Harris, John, *A Catalogue of British Drawings for Architecture, Decoration, Sculpture and Landscape Gardening, 1550-1900, in American Collections*, The Gregg Press, 1971

8 | Further reading

The most comprehensive bibliography of publications describing historic parks and gardens remains Ray Desmond's *Bibliography of British Gardens* (1988). A supplementary *Bibliography of Garden History* has been prepared by Desmond, and was published in *Garden History* 18:1 (Spring 1990), and the Garden History Society continues to publish regular bibliographies of new books and articles. The further reading, below, supplies some particularly useful references not already mentioned as well as many that have, some of the basic reference books included in Desmond (most of which contain further references and bibliographies), and a number of books which have appeared since Desmond.

Reference books and guides to sources

Barley MW, *A Guide to British Topographical Collections*, Council for British Archaeology, 1974

Brodie, Antonia; Felstead, Alison; Franklin, Jonathan, et al [RIBA], *Directory of British Architects, 1834-1914*, 2 vols, Continuum International, 2001

Burke, Bernard, *Burke's Genealogical and Heraldic History of the Peerage, Baronetage and Knightage*, Burke's Peerage, London, 107th edition, 2003

Burke, Bernard, *Burke's Genealogical and Heraldic History of the Landed Gentry*, 1-19 editions, Burke's Peerage, London, 1833-2005

Cadw, *Register of Landscapes, Parks and Gardens of Special Historic Interest in Wales*, 2002. Websites: *www.cadw.wales.gov.uk* and *www.ccw.gov.uk*

Colvin, Howard, *A Biographical Dictionary of British Architects 1600-1840*, Paul Mellon, 1997

Desmond, Ray, *A Bibliography of British Gardens*, St Paul's Bibliographies, 1988

Desmond, Ray, 'A Bibliography of Garden History', *Garden History*, 18:1, Garden History Society, 1990

Desmond, Ray and Ellwood, Christine, *A Dictionary of British and Irish Botanists and Horticulturists including Plant Collectors, Flower Painters and Garden Designers*, Taylor & Francis, 1994

Elton, EA, Harrison, B and Wark, K, *Researching the Country House: a Guide for Local Historians*, Batsford, 1993

Evans, Eric J, *Tithes: Maps, Apportionments and the 1836 Act*, British Association for Local History, 1993

Foster, Janet and Sheppard, Julia [eds], *British Archives: a Guide to Archive Resources in the United Kingdom*, Macmillan, 2000

Garden History Society, *Register of Research*, Garden History Society, 2002, *www.gardenhistorysociety.org/ researchregister.htm*

Goldman, L [ed], *The Oxford Dictionary of National Biography*, Oxford University Press, 2004

Goode, Patrick, Lancaster, Michael [eds], *The Oxford Companion to Gardens*, Oxford University Press, 2001

Gray, Stuart A, *Edwardian Architecture: a biographical dictionary*, Wandsworth Editions, 1988

Harley, JB, *The Historian's Guide to Ordnance Survey Maps*, London, for the Standing Conference for Local History by the National Council of Social Service, 1964

Harley, JB, *Maps for the Local Historian: a guide to the British sources*, for the Standing Conference for Local History by the National Council of Social Service, 1972

Hindle, Paul, *Maps for Historians*, Phillimore, 1998

Harris, John, *A Catalogue of British Drawings for Architecture, Decoration, Sculpture and Landscape Gardening, 1550-1900 in American Collections*, New Jersey, Gregg Press, 1971; a useful guide to British material in the extensive manuscript collections of American Museums, galleries, libraries and universities

Harris, John, *Country House Index*, Pinhorns, 1979

Harris, John, *The Artist and the Country House from the Fifteenth Century to the Present Day*, Sotheby's, 1996

Harvey, John, *Sources for the History of Houses*, British Records Association, 1974

Holmes, Michael [ed], *The Country House Described*, St Paul's Bibliographies, 1986

Jupp, B [ed], *Heritage Gardens Inventory*, Environment and Heritage Service Northern Ireland, 1992

Kain, RJP and Prince, HC, *The Tithe Surveys of England and Wales*, Cambridge University Press, 1985

Kamen RH [ed], *British and Irish Architectural Sources, A Bibliography and Guide to Sources of Information*, Architectural Press, 1981

Pevsner, Nikolaus, *The Buildings of England; The Buildings of Scotland; The Buildings of Ireland; The Buildings of Wales*, Penguin Books, Harmondsworth, 1951-. The modern editions and revisions contain useful material on the grounds of the houses described. See also *A Compendium of Pevsner's Buildings of England* on CD, Oxford University Press, 1995

Prince, Hugh, *Parks in England*, Pinhorns, 1967; includes a list of places where a number of known designers worked, and a list of engravings by Kip, Badeslade etc

Scottish Natural Heritage and Historic Scotland, *An Inventory of Gardens and Designed Landscapes in Scotland*, Glasgow, 1997; supplementary volumes 2001 and 2003

Smith, David, *Maps and Plans for the Local Historian*, Batsford, 1988

Taylor, Patrick [ed], *The Oxford Companion to the Garden*, Oxford University Press, 2006

The Victoria History of the Counties of England, over 200 vols, London, 1899-. Website: *www.englandpast.net*; some volumes published electronically at *www.british-history.ac.uk*

Fieldwork

Brown, AE, *Garden Archaeology*, Council for British Archaeology Research Report no. 78, 1991

Currie, Christopher, *Garden Archaeology: A Handbook*, Practical Handbooks in Archaeology, Council for British Archaeology, 2005

Jacques, David, 'The techniques and uses of garden archaeology', *Journal of Garden History* vol.17, no.1, Jan-Mar 1997

Mitchell, Alan, *A Field Guide to the Trees of Britain and Northern Europe*, Collins, London, 1974; includes a rough guide to dating trees, and dates of introductions for ornamental species

National Trust, 'A survey of the gardens and park at Belton', vol iii, pp 3-7, 1986; contains a more refined method of dating trees. Available at the University of York, and the RHS Lindley Library.

Pattison, Paul [ed], 'There by Design: field archaeology in parks and gardens', *British Archaeological Reports*, 267, 1998

Phibbs, JL, 'An Approach to the methodology of recording historic gardens', *Garden History* 11:2, Autumn 1983

Rackham, Oliver, *Trees and Woodland in the British Landscape*, Weidenfeld & Nicholson, 2001

Rackham, Oliver, *The History of the Countryside*, Weidenfeld & Nicholson, 2000

Royal Commission on the Ancient and Historical Monuments and Construction of England, *An inventory of the historical monuments in... A number of inventories for different counties*, HMSO, 1910-85

Williamson, Tom, 'The Archaeology of the Landscape Park: garden design in Norfolk', c. 1680-1840, *British Archaeological Reports*, 268, 1998

Photographs

Evans, Hilary and Mary, *The Picture Researcher's Handbook*, 8th editon, 2006

Kamen, Ruth H, *British and Irish Architectural History: A Bibliography and Guide to Sources of Information*, Architectural Press, 1981; contains a directory of photograph and slide libraries

Wall, John [ed], *The Directory of British Photographic Collections*, RPS/Heinemann, 1977; contains a list of agencies and libraries and notes the speciality of each

Grannum, Karen, *Pocket Guide to Family History: Using Wills*, National Archives, 2000

Grannum, Karen and Taylor, Nigel, *Wills and Other Probate Records*, National Archives, 2004

Marshall, Hilary, *Palaeography for Family and Local Historians*, Phillimore, 2004

Selected monographs and articles on garden design and designers

Design

Batey, Mavis, *Regency Gardens*, Shire Publications, 1995

Brooks, Chris, *Mortal Remains: the history and present state of the Victorian and Edwardian Cemetery*, Wheaton with the association of the Victorian Society, Exeter, 1989

Brown, Jane, *The English Garden in our Time: From Gertrude Jekyll to Geoffrey Jellicoe*, Antique Collectors' Club, 1986

Brown, Jane, *The English Garden through the 20th Century*, Garden Art Press, 1999

Brown, Jane, *The Modern Garden*, Thames and Hudson, 2001

Campbell, Susan, *Charleston Kedding: a history of kitchen gardening*, Ebury Press, 1996

Cantor, LM, *The Medieval Parks of England: a Gazetteer*, Dept of Education, Loughborough University, 1983

Chambers, Douglas, *The Planters of the English Landscape Garden*, Yale University Press, 1993

Conner, Patrick, *Oriental architecture in the west*, Thames and Hudson, 1979

Conway, Hazel, *People's Parks: the design and development of Victorian parks in Britain*, Shire Publications, 1996

Conway, Hazel, 'Everyday Landscapes: public parks from 1930-2000', *Garden History*, 28:1, Garden History Society, Summer 2000

Crouch, David and Ward, Colin, *The Allotment: its landscape and culture*, Five Leaves Publications, 1997

Elliott, Brent, *Victorian Gardens*, Timber Press, 1986

Elliott, Brent, *The Country House Garden: from the archives of Country Life 1897-1939*, Mitchell Beazley, 1995

Davis, John, *Antique Garden Ornament*, Antique Collectors' Club, 1991

Fleming, Laurence and Gore, Alan, *The English Garden*, Michael Joseph, 1982

Hadfield, Miles; Harling, Robert; Highton, Leonie [eds], *British Gardeners: A biographical dictionary*, Zwemmer, 1985

Hadfield, Miles, *A History of British Gardening*, Penguin Books, 1985

Harding, Jane and Taigel, Anthea, 'An Air of Detachment: town gardens in the eighteenth and nineteenth centuries', *Garden History* 24:2, Garden History Society, 1996

Headley, Gwyn and Meulenkamp, Wim, *Follies, Grottoes and Garden Buildings*, Aurum Press, 1999

Hix, John, *The Glasshouse*, Phaidon Press, 2005

Hunt, John Dixon, *Garden and grove: the Italian Renaissance garden in the English imagination*, JM Dent, 1986

Hussey, Christopher, *English Gardens and Landscapes 1700-1750*, Country Life, 1967

Jacques, David, *Georgian Gardens: the reign of Nature*, Timber Press, 1984

Jacques, David and van der Horst, Arend Jan [eds], *The gardens of William and Mary*, BT Batsford, 1991

Jones, Barbara, *Follies and Grottoes*, Constable and Robinson, 1974

Jordan, Harriet, 'Public Parks, 1885-1914', *Garden History*, 22:1, *Garden History Society*, Summer, 1994

Longstaffe-Gowan, Todd, *The London Town Garden 1700-1840*, Yale University Press, 2001

Loudon, John Claudius, *An Encyclopaedia of Gardening*, Longman, 1822

Meller, Hugh, *London Cemeteries: an illustrated guide and gazetteer*, Ashgate, 1994

Ottewill, David, *The Edwardian Garden*, Yale University Press, 1989

Roberts, Jane, *Royal Landscape: the gardens and parks of Windsor*, Yale University Press, 1997

Roberts, J, and Currie, E, *A Survey of the Historic Parks and Gardens of Greater Manchester*, Greater Manchester Archaeological Unit, Manchester University and the Institute of Advanced Architectural Studies, the University of York, 1994

Rutherford, Sarah, 'The Landscapes of Public Lunatic Asylums in England, 1808-1914', unpublished PhD thesis, De Montfort University, 2003

Shirley, Evelyn Philip, *Some Account of English Deer Parks* Deer Study and Resource Centre, 2005

Strong, Roy, *The Renaissance Garden in England*, Thames and Hudson, 1984

Symes, Michael, *A Glossary of Garden History*, Shire Publications, 1993

Taylor, Hilary A, 'Urban Public Parks, 1840-1900: design and meaning', *Garden History*, 23:2, Garden History Society, Winter 1995

Whitaker, Joseph, *A Descriptive List of the Deer Parks and Paddocks of England*, 1892

Worpole, Ken, *Last Landscapes: the architecture of the cemetery in the west*, Reaktion, 2003

Woudstra, Jan [ed], 'Reviewing the Twentieth-Century Landscape', *Garden History* 28:1 (2000)

Woudstra, Jan and Fieldhouse, Ken [eds], *The Regeneration of Public Parks*, The Garden History Society, Landscape Design Trust and E & FN Spon with the support of English Heritage, London, 2000

Designers

Batey, Mavis, *Alexander Pope: the Poet and the Landscape*, Barn Elms Publishing, 1999

Brown, Jane, *Gardens of a Golden Afternoon: The Story of a Partnership, Edward Lutyens and Gertrude Jekyll*, Allen Lane, 1982

Brown, Jane, *Eminent Gardeners*, Viking, 1990

Brown, Jane, *Lanning Roper and his Gardens*, Rizzoli, 1987

Carter, George; Goode, Patrick; Laurie, Kedrun, *Humphry Repton Landscape Gardener 1752-1818*, Sainsbury Centre, 1982

Collens, Geoffrey and Powell, Wendy [eds], *Sylvia Crowe*, Landscape Design Trust, 1999

Colquhoun, Kate, *A Thing in Disguise: the visionary life of Joseph Paxton*, Harper Perennial, 2003

Cowell, Fiona, 'Richard Woods (?1716-93): a preliminary account', *Garden History* 14:2, Autumn 1986 and 15:2, Autumn 1987

Daniels, Stephen, *Humphry Repton: landscape gardening and the geography of Georgian England*, Yale University Press, 1999

Desmond, Ray, and Ellwood, Christine, *Dictionary of British and Irish Botanists and Horticulturists*, Taylor and Francis, 1994

Downs Annabel [ed], *Peter Shepheard*, Landscape Design Trust, 2004

Green, David, *Gardener to Queen Anne: Henry Wise (1653-1738)*, Oxford University Press, 1956

John Claudius Loudon and the Early Nineteenth Century in Great Britain, papers from the sixth Dumbarton Oaks Colloquium on the History of Landscape, Washington DC, 1980

Harris, Eileen, *Thomas Wright: Arbours and Grottos*, Solar Press, 1979

Harris, John, *William Chambers, Knight of the Polar Star*, Zwemmer, 1970

Harvey, Sheila, *Geoffrey Jellicoe*, Landscape Design Trust, 1998

Hunt, John Dixon , *William Kent: Landscape Garden Designer*, Zwemmer, 1987

Loudon JC, *The landscape gardening and landscape architecture of the late Humphry Repton Esq*, Longman, London, 1840. Repton's published writings, with an invaluable index.

Jordan, Harriet , 'Thomas Hayton Mawson (1861-1933), The English Gardens of an Edwardian landscape architect', unpublished PhD thesis, London University, Wye College, 1988

Piebenga, Sophieke, 'William Sawrey Gilpin (1762-1843: picturesque improver', *Garden History*, 22:2, 1994

Ridgway, Christopher and Williams, Robert, [eds], *Sir John Vanbrugh and Landscape Architecture in Baroque England, 1690-1730*, Suttons, Stroud, 2000

Simo, Melanie Louise , *Loudon and the Landscape: from Country Seat to Metropolis 1783-1843*, Yale University Press, 1988

Spens, Michael, *The Complete Landscape Designs and Gardens of Geoffrey Jellicoe*, Thames and Hudson, 1994

Stroud, Dorothy, *Capability Brown*, Faber and Faber, 1975

Turnbull, Deborah, 'Thomas White: 18th-century landscape designer and arboriculturist', unpublished PhD, Hull University, 1990

Wilkinson, Anne, 'The Preternatural Gardener: the life of James Shirley Hibberd', *Garden History*, 26:2, 1998

Willis, Peter, *Charles Bridgeman and the English Landscape Garden*, Elysium Press, Newcastle upon Tyne, 1977, revised 2002

Wilson, Michael, *William Kent, Architect, Designer, Painter, Gardener 1685-1748*, London, 1984

Woudstra, Jan [ed], 'Lancelot Brown (1716-83) and the Landscape Park', *Garden History*, 29:1 (2001)

Local and other regional studies

An increasing number of local or regional surveys or studies are now being published. Those given below represent a selection of these works:

Anderson, AP, *The Captain and the Norwich Parks*, The Norwich Society, 2000

Bond, James, *Somerset Parks and Gardens: a landscape history*, Somerset Books, 1998

Buxbaum, Tim, *Scottish Garden Buildings: from food to folly*, Mainstream, 1989

Register of Landscapes, Parks and Gardens of Special Historic Interest in Wales, Cadw, 2002. Visit: *www.cadw.wales.gov.uk* and *www.ccw.gov.uk*

Edwards, Mervyn, *Potters in Parks*, Churnet Valley Books, 1999

Cambridgeshire Gardens Trust, *The Gardens of Cambridgeshire: a Gazetteer*, Cambridgeshire , 2000

Galinou, Mireille [ed], *London's Pride: the glorious history of the capital's gardens*, Anaya, 1990

Harding, Stewart and Lambert, David, *Parks and Gardens of Avon*, Avon Gardens Trust, 1994

Hedley, Gill and Rance, Adrian, *Pleasure Grounds; the Gardens and Landscapes of Hampshire*, Milestone, 1987

Hertfordshire Gardens Trust and Williamson, Tom, *The Parks and Gardens of West Hertfordshire*, Hertfordshire Gardens Trust, 2000

Howley, James, *The Follies and Garden Buildings of Ireland*, Yale University Press, 1993

Lockett, Richard, *A Survey of Historic Parks and Gardens in Worcestershire*, Hereford and Worcester Gardens Trust, 1997

Mowl, Timothy, *The Historic Gardens of Gloucestershire*, Tempus Publishing, 2002. This is the first of a project intended to cover all the counties of England, and subsequent volumes (Dorset, 2003, and Cornwall, 2005) have appeared regularly

Neave, David and Turnbull, Deborah, *Landscaped Parks and Gardens of East Yorkshire*, Garden Society for East Yorkshire, 1992

Pett, Douglas Ellery, and HRH The Prince of Wales, *Parks and Gardens of Cornwall: A Companion Guide Arranged to Correspond with the Ordnance Survey Landranger Maps*, Alison Hodge Publishers, 1998

Pugsley, Stephen [ed], *Devon Gardens: a historical survey*, Alan Sutton, 1994

Scott, Robert, *A Breath of Fresh Air: the Story of Belfast's Parks*, Blackstaff, 2000

Sheeran, George, *Landscape gardens in West Yorkshire 1680-1880*, King's England Press, 1990

Stamper, Paul, Historic Parks and Gardens of Shropshire, Shropshire Books, 1996

Tait, AA, *The Landscape Garden in Scotland, 1735-1835*, Edinburgh University Press, 1980

Whitehead, David and Paton, Jane [ed], *A Survey of Historic Parks and Gardens in Herefordshire*, Hereford and Worcester Gardens Trust, 2001

Williamson, Tom, 'The Archaeology of the Landscape Park: garden design in Norfolk, c. 1680-1840', *British Archaeological Reports*, 268, 1998

Williamson, Tom, *Suffolk's Gardens and Parks: designed landscapes from the Tudors to the Victorians*, Windgather, 2000

Wilson-North, Robert , [ed], *The Lie of the Land: aspects of the archaeology and history of the designed landscape in the South West of England*, The Mint Press and the Devon Gardens Trust, 2003

Diaries and tours

There is a growing literature of travel and tourism. The following texts are useful in supplying bibliographical references to primary texts.

Andrews, Malcolm, *The Search for the Picturesque: landscape aesthetics and tourism in Britain, 1760-1800*, Scholar Press, 1989

Batey, Mavis and Lambert, David, *The English Garden Tour*, John Murray, 1990

Cox, EG, *Reference Guide to the Literature of Travel…Great Britain*, vol iii, University of Washington Press, 1949

Fussell, GS, *The Exploration of England: A select bibliography of travel and topography, 1570-1815*, 1935

Mitchell, Arthur, *Lists of Travels and Tours in Scotland 1296 to 1900*, Edinburgh, 1902

Esther Moir, *The Discovery of Britain: The English tourists, 1540-1840*, Routledge & Kegan Paul, 1964

Ian Ousby, *The Englishman's England: taste, travel and the rise of tourism*, Cambridge University Press, 1990

Journals and magazines

Journals and magazines are a valuable source of information on garden history. One useful index to modern academic journals, and a source of abstracts, is the British Humanities Index (Library Association, London, 1962). A descriptive list of Victorian gardening magazines was published by Ray Desmond in Garden History 5:3 (Winter 1977).

Useful modern journals include:

Country Life (1897-); annual cumulative index available

Garden History (1972-) and GHS Quarterly Newsletter, 1966-72. Indexes available on *www.gardenhistorysociety.org*

Journal of Garden History, formerly *Studies in the History of Gardens and Designed Landscapes* (1981-). Abstracts in *British Humanities Index (qv)*

Landscape Design (now incorporated in *Green Places*), the official journal of the Landscape Institute, 1934- 2003

Landscape, the official journal of the Landscape Institute, 2004-

Early journals and magazines of particular interest include:

The Gentleman's Magazine, contemporary indexes available

The Gardener's Magazine (1826-44) ed. JC London

The Gardeners' Chronicle (1841-1983)

Cottage Gardener (1848-61), continued as Journal of Horticulture, *Cottage Gardener* … (1861-1915)

The last four publications and many others have been indexed in Desmond, 1988

Picture acknowledgments

The publishers would like to thank the following for their kind permission in allowing use of their images:

pages 11, 12, 14, 16 (top), 18, 19, 21, 28, 36, 38
English Heritage

page 16 (below)
English Heritage/Andrew Turner

page 20
English Heritage/Tim Walker

pages 30, 39
English Heritage/Tony Bartholomew

page 32
English Heritage/Jeremy Richards

page 30
English Heritage/Deborah Cunliffe

page 23
Reproduced by kind permission of The British Library

page 26
Courtesy of the Trustees of the William Salt Library, Stafford

page 27
City of London, London Metropolitan Archives

page 29
By permission of Llyfrgell Genedlaethol Cymru/ The National Library of Wales, reference DV66f64

page 33
Gwent Record Office, reference D43.4798

page 35
Gloucestershire Archives, reference D1388 Box 91

page 31 (left)
Parks Agency

page 31 (right)
City of Bradford Metropolitan Borough Council